English for the Financial Sector

Teacher's Book

Ian MacKenzie

CAMBRIDGE
UNIVERSITY PRESS

CAMBRIDGE UNIVERSITY PRESS
Cambridge, New York, Melbourne, Madrid, Cape Town,
Singapore, São Paulo, Delhi, Tokyo, Mexico City

Cambridge University Press
The Edinburgh Building, Cambridge CB2 8RU, UK

www.cambridge.org
Information on this title: www.cambridge.org/9780521547260

First published 2008
4th printing 2012

A catalogue record for this publication is available from the British Library

ISBN 978-0-521-54725-3 Student's Book
ISBN 978-0-521-54726-0 Teacher's Book
ISBN 978-0-521-54728-4 CD (audio)

Cambridge University Press has no responsibility for the persistence or
accuracy of URLs for external or third-party internet websites referred to in
this publication, and does not guarantee that any content on such websites is,
or will remain, accurate or appropriate. Information regarding prices, travel
timetables and other factual information given in this work is correct at
the time of first printing but Cambridge University Press does not guarantee
the accuracy of such information thereafter.

Contents

Student's Book Content

Unit	Vocabulary	Reading	Listening	Language focus	Speaking	Writing
1	The organization of the financial industry	Key vocabulary of banking products and services	Regulation and deregulation	The development of the financial industry; Going international	Permission, necessity and prohibition	Role play: Bank account terms and conditions	
2	Telephoning			Arranging meetings; Handling information	Pronouncing the alphabet and saying telephone numbers	Role plays: Arranging meetings, Asking for information	
3	Retail banking	Key vocabulary of retail banking	Commercial and investment banking; The future of bank branches	Retail banking	Likelihood and probability	Role play: Should we invest in our branches?	
4	Business correspondence 1	Email and web addresses			Formal and informal style 1	Email etiquette	Emails
5	Loans and credit	Key vocabulary of loans and credit	Banks and bonds	Lending decisions; Margins	Advising and suggesting	Role plays: Lending decisions, Advising on bank products and services	Email summarizing a meeting
6	Business correspondence 2			A letter of complaint; An angry phone call	Formal and informal style 2		Replying to a letter of complaint; Responding to a phone call; Apologizing

Unit		Vocabulary	Reading	Listening	Language focus	Speaking	Writing
7	Accounting	Key vocabulary of financial statements and accounting		Types of accounting; Financial statements; Barclays' balance sheet	Talking about figures 1	Role play: Presenting financial statements	
8	Socializing			Greeting people and making introductions; Talking about your career; Saying goodbye	Making small talk and keeping the conversation going	Role plays: Greeting visitors and making small talk, Talking about your career, Saying goodbye	
9	Central banking	Key vocabulary of central banking and monetary policy	The Bank of England	Monetary policy; Saying figures	Talking about figures 2	Central banking decisions	
10	Meetings 1	Key vocabulary of meetings		Chairing a meeting; Interruptions and digressions	Controlling meetings	Role play: A meeting	
11	Financing international trade	Key vocabulary of letters of credit and bills of exchange	How a letter of credit works	Asking for information about bills of exchange	Checking and confirming information	Role play: Clarifying Incoterms	
12	Meetings 2	Word combinations relating to meetings		Concluding a meeting	Asking for and giving opinions, agreeing and disagreeing	Expressing opinions Role play: Outsourcing a call centre	Email summarizing action points

Unit		Vocabulary	Reading	Listening	Language focus	Speaking	Writing
13	Foreign exchange	Key vocabulary of exchange rates	Exchange rates; Currency trading	Freely floating exchange rates	Describing trends and graphs	Describing a graph	
14	Writing reports 1	Vocabulary to describe reasons, consequences and contrasts	Facts and opinions		Linking words		Findings and recommendations; A report on a trade finance website
15	Stocks and shares	Key vocabulary of the stock market	Why stock markets matter	A financial market report	Understanding market reports	Describing and drawing a graph; Discussing a portfolio	
16	Writing reports 2		Head office relocation	Catering choices; Health and leisure needs	Style and tone		A report on facilities in the new head office
17	Mergers and acquisitions	Key vocabulary of mergers, takeovers and buyouts	Mergers, takeovers and buyouts	The role of banks	Cause and effect	Describing cause and effect Role play: A takeover bid	Summarizing a meeting
18	Negotiating 1		Learn to Love Negotiating	Conditional offers; Should we grant this loan?	Making proposals, counter-proposals and conditional offers	Role plays: Making proposals and conditional offers, Negotiating a loan	Summarizing a negotiation

Unit		Vocabulary	Reading	Listening	Language focus	Speaking	Writing
19	Derivatives	Key vocabulary of derivatives	Derivatives; An investment 'time bomb'	Derivatives	Clarifying, summarizing and paraphrasing	Defending or criticizing derivatives	
20	Negotiating 2			Concluding an unsuccessful negotiation; Concluding a successful negotiation; Saturday opening	Dealing with conflict	Role play: Negotiating Saturday opening	
21	Asset management	Key vocabulary of asset management and allocation	Fund management	Asset management and allocation; Investment styles	Using diplomatic language	Role play: Disagreeing diplomatically	Email summarizing a meeting; A letter of complaint
22	Presentations 1		Learning styles	The introduction	Visual aids	Preparing an introduction	
23	Regulating the financial sector		Conflicts of interest	The FSA; Conflicts of interest	Word formation	Ethical choices	
24	Presentations 2			Parts of a presentation; The end of a presentation	Dealing with questions and troubleshooting	Beginning and ending the parts of a presentation; The ending of a presentation; A complete presentation	

Introduction

English for the Financial Sector consists of a Student's Book, two audio CDs, and this Teacher's Book. The Student's Book contains 24 units, tapescripts, a word list, and file cards for the speaking activities in the units.

Who is *English for the Financial Sector* for?

English for the Financial Sector is a course for business students and people working in the financial industry with an intermediate or upper-intermediate level of English (Common European Framework for Languages levels B1/B2 and upwards).

How long is it?

The course provides approximately 50 hours of lessons. Each of the 24 units should take between 1.5 and 2.5 hours of class time. Some of the material can also be done as self-study or homework.

Aims of the course

The course aims to:

- cover the basic concepts of most areas of finance (retail banking, investment banking, securities, asset management, central banking, foreign exchange, international trade, accounting, financial regulation and supervision, etc.)
- build financial vocabulary through reading, listening and discussion
- develop comprehension of financial texts
- develop listening skills, using interviews with financial professionals
- improve speaking skills through discussion, case studies and role plays
- develop business communication proficiency by increasing learners' confidence and fluency in a range of skills
- practise specific language functions such as advising, suggesting, agreeing and disagreeing, clarifying, reviewing, summarizing.

The two types of units

The odd-numbered units are **content-based**, usually containing an authentic interview with someone working in the financial sector, as well as a short text, often from an authentic source. The original interviews have been rerecorded to make comprehension easier, but the wording is very close to the original. The interviewees include the former director of the Bank of England's Centre for Central Banking Studies, a member of the Bank of England's Monetary Policy Committee, a financial director, an investment consultant, and people from a range of banking backgrounds. Between them, the interviews and texts give an overview of a particular area of finance, introduce essential concepts, and have a high density of specialized vocabulary. They are accompanied by comprehension and **Vocabulary** exercises, **Discussion** topics and case studies, and **Practice** activities allowing learners to use key language in a real or typical context.

The even-numbered units practise **business communication skills**, in a financial context: telephoning, writing emails, letters and reports, socializing, participating in meetings, negotiating, and making presentations.

Each unit has a **Language focus** section looking at a specific language area. Clear examples are followed by practice exercises to help consolidate learning.

The listening material includes British, American, European and Indian speakers. **Tapescripts** of all the listening material are also included at the back of the **Student's Book**.

Pair and group work

Virtually all the exercises and activities are designed to be done by pairs or small groups of learners. Where the instructions do not specify '… in pairs or small groups', this should be taken as implicit. Many of the exercises and activities can also be done as self-study. In one-to-one lessons, you can adapt the **Practice** role plays, with the teacher taking one of the roles. Recording the activity can help with feedback.

Teaching pre-service and in-service learners

If your learners already work in finance, they will be able to bring their knowledge and experience to bear on the activities and exercises. If your learners are full-time business students who have not yet worked in finance, they might have studied the subject-matter in their own language. The trick of teaching specialized forms of a language is, of course, to use the learner as a resource whenever possible. If your learners know more than you about a subject, elicit information from them. It would be possible to begin many of the units by eliciting information about the topic from the learners, with their books closed.

Finding out more about finance

There is a **Background** containing additional information in most of the content units in this Teacher's Book. Although these units endeavour to cover the basic concepts and terminology of finance, both learners and teachers may want to search for further information, definitions, etc. Students requiring further information about finance, and exercises designed for self-study, might be interested in *Professional English in Use Finance* (Cambridge University Press, 2006).

There are a number of comprehensive financial glossaries available on the internet, including (at the time of writing – internet addresses can and do change):

> http://www.investorwords.com/
> http://www.finance-glossary.com/pages/home.htm
> http://biz.yahoo.com/f/g/
> http://www.bloomberg.com/invest/glossary/bfglosa.htm
> http://www.forbes.com/tools/glossary/index.jhtml
> http://www.nytimes.com/library/financial/glossary/bfglosa.htm
> http://www.ubs.com/1/e/about/bterms.html
> http://tradition.axone.ch/

The last two glossaries in this list are in English, French, German and Italian.

For definitions, try typing *define* followed by a colon and the word you want defined into Google, for example, *define:bond*.

For more detailed but accessible explanations of financial terms and concepts, I recommend three books published by *The Economist* in association with Profile Books, London: *Pocket Accounting* (Christopher Nobes), *Pocket Finance* (Tim Hindle) and *Pocket Investor* (Philip Ryland). Most of the other books in this series would also be useful to business English teachers.

The Cambridge International Certificate in Financial English

This is a new examination in financial English skills for finance and accounting professionals, at levels B2 and C1 of the Common European Framework for Languages, developed by University of Cambridge ESOL Examinations (English for Speakers of Other Languages) and ACCA (the Association of Chartered Certified Accountants).

The Cambridge ICFE exam consists of four papers: the Test of Reading; the Test of Writing; the Test of Listening and the Test of Speaking. All the texts and tasks concern finance and accounting topics. See:

> http://www.financialenglish.org/

and

> http://www.cambridgeesol.org/teach/icfe/index.html

English for the Financial Sector covers many of the topic areas included in the examination, and provides practice in the skills required for the four different Tests.

I hope you enjoy using this book with your learners.

1 The organization of the financial industry

AIMS

To learn about: types of banks; the organization of the financial industry; key vocabulary of banking products and services
To learn how to: express permission, necessity and prohibition
To practise: asking and talking about terms and conditions of bank accounts

BACKGROUND: THE FINANCIAL SECTOR

The financial sector (or the financial services industry) includes the following areas, most of which are covered in this book:

- commercial banks, which receive customers' deposits and make loans
- private banks, which manage the assets of wealthy individuals
- investment banks, which advise and raise money for companies, and sell and trade financial products
- investment companies, which invest customers' money in funds and other companies
- the money markets, in which financial institutions, companies and government bodies can borrow and invest in the short-term (less than one year)
- the currency markets, in which individuals and companies can buy and sell foreign currency
- the stock market, where the stocks and shares of public companies are traded
- the futures and derivatives markets, where these financial instruments are traded
- the inter-bank clearing system, in which financial institutions settle credits and debits among themselves
- insurance companies, which offer financial protection against risks such as accidents, fire, theft, loss, damage, etc.
- accounting and auditing companies, which examine companies' financial records to make sure they are accurate and in accordance with the law
- regulatory authorities, which ensure that financial institutions and markets comply with laws and regulations.

This unit outlines the recent history of the financial industry, and the way in which recent deregulation has led to formerly separate financial organizations – commercial banks, investment banks, stockbroking houses, insurance companies, etc. – combining to form large financial institutions.

Lead in

The lead-in for each unit provides discussion questions as a way into the unit. Anyone old enough to study finance is likely to have a bank account. If you don't have any learners already working in financial institutions, the discussion may be less varied. However, learners could think about any changes they have noticed in recent years as bank customers.

As with nearly all the exercises and activities in this course (except those for small groups), this activity is probably best done in pairs, followed by a short discussion, or question and answer session, with the whole class. (If you are teaching one-to-one, try to elicit as much information as you can from your student.)

Vocabulary 1

As with many exercises in this book, learners can either do this in pairs or complete it on their own and then check their answers together when they've finished. There is an answer key in the **Student's Book**, but it would be a good idea to ask the learners <u>not</u> to consult it before you have elicited answers from the class.

ANSWERS

1 mortgage	5 capital
2 deposit	6 bonds
3 pension	7 takeover
4 stocks, shares	8 merger

VOCABULARY NOTES

American English tends to use the word *stock* while British English uses the word *share*, though British English uses *stock* in compounds such as *stock market*, *stock exchange*, *stockbroker*, *stock option*, etc. (See **Unit 15**, Stocks and shares)

The most common use of *stock* in British English is to refer to the total amount of goods or the amount of a particular type of goods available for sale at a particular time (*inventory* in American English).

Takeover is a noun; the verb is in two words (*to*) *take over* (see **Unit 17**).

Listening 1: The development of the financial industry

You will probably need to play this recording – and most of the others in this course – twice. The learners can read the questions, listen a first time, try to answer the questions, check their answers in pairs, and listen a second time to confirm their answers, before you elicit answers from the class. Depending on the level of the learners, and the difficulty of the recording, playing the recording a third time may also be necessary. Learners should be actively discouraged from reading the tapescripts at the back of the **Student's Book** before listening, or while listening for the first time.

Here, and in other listening comprehension exercises based on authentic materials, quotes from the script have been included in order to help you explain / justify the answers. Students should also be encouraged to give explanations for their answers.

🔘 **1.1** TAPESCRIPT

Peter Sinclair: Well, twenty-five years ago the financial industry in most countries had two key characteristics. One was that pretty well all the banks and financial institutions in that country were owned in that country, and there were few international links – in many cases none. So they were national banks belonging to that country. The other key feature was that financial institutions were specialized, so in Britain we had institutions that lent to people who wanted to borrow to buy houses – that means arranging mortgages – so we had specialized things called building societies doing that. We had retail banks where individuals and companies kept bank deposits and which made loans to cover short-term outlays and in some cases longer-term investment. Then we had another range of institutions like insurance companies to provide life insurance or pensions, and we had investment banks – sometimes called merchant banks. These weren't retail banks; they didn't deal with individuals, they dealt with big companies. They gave the companies financial advice, maybe arranging mergers, or fighting off a takeover bid, and helped to raise capital, for example by issuing shares or bonds.

NOTES

Shortly after this recording was made, Peter Sinclair left the Centre for Central Banking Studies at the Bank of England, and returned to Birmingham University where he is Professor of Economics.

Further extracts from this interview are used in **Units 3**, **13**, **17** and **19**.

With more advanced learners, you could point out (or let them identify) *key*, a synonym for 'very important' that Sinclair uses twice, and *pretty well*, a phrase meaning 'nearly (all)' or 'almost (all)'. He also uses the noun *outlay*, meaning amounts of money spent for particular purposes.

Listening 2: Going international

As with other listening exercises in this book, you can ask learners to predict answers before listening. They can discuss their predictions in pairs then listen a first time to see if their predictions were correct, compare their answers in pairs, and listen again to confirm the correct answers. If learners feel they have the answers at this stage you can elicit them from the class. If a third listening is requested by the learners, try to ensure that they have a slightly different task, e.g. elicit the answers they are happy with first, so they just focus on the problem question(s) for the third listening.

🔘 1.2 TAPESCRIPT

Peter Sinclair: In the old days in Britain, the merchant or investment banks were pretty well all British and there were big boundaries between building societies and insurance companies and all these other types of companies. Well, now if you look at the picture, many banks have become universal banks; perhaps 'banks' is the wrong word. Lots of institutions do all the things that I have just described – insurance, mortgages, advice, raising capital for companies, and retail banking besides, and the other great change is that so many of the financial institutions – and it is not just true of Britain, true of pretty much everywhere else – are now international. So, for example in Britain, two of the big four retail banks have changed ownership: one was taken over by Hong Kong and Shanghai Bank, that was the Midland Bank previously, and it's now changed its name to Hong Kong and Shanghai Bank and it really isn't a British bank any more; and another, National Westminster, was taken over by the Royal Bank of Scotland. But if you look at, say, countries like the Czech Republic or Hungary or Poland or New Zealand too, and plenty of other small countries around the world, all their financial institutions pretty well are now owned by foreigners, by German companies, or French companies or Austrian companies – whatever it might be – and the huge international financial institutions are typically, though not all of them, American; and you can now think of the City of London, the world's leading centre for foreign exchange dealings and a great deal of finance, as rather like Wimbledon. In other words it's a great big international stage, happens to be in London, but most of the players are foreign; they are nearly all foreign companies that do, for example, the investment banking and so many other things.

So internationalization and, if you like, homogenization of these hitherto specialized financial institutions. Those are the two big recent trends.

ANSWERS
1 Many banks have become international, by buying banks in other countries or through being taken over.
2 The City of London is a major financial centre, but most of the banks operating there are not British, just as Wimbledon is a big international tennis tournament that takes place in London, although very few of the players are British.
3 Internationalization and homogenization (making all the banks become the same, or very similar).

VOCABULARY NOTES

Sinclair again uses *pretty well*, as well as a synonym, *pretty much*. He also uses the phrase *if you look at the picture* meaning 'look at the current situation'. He describes the major participants or companies in the finance industry as *players*, which is a common idiom, and uses *hitherto*, a fairly formal alternative to 'previously'.

Discussion

This is a good opportunity to relate what Sinclair says to students' personal experience. There may be examples of recent mergers or takeovers of banks in their countries.

Vocabulary 2

It is always worth drawing learners' attention to common verb–noun word combinations (also known as word partnerships, or collocations), as nouns are generally used with an accompanying verb, and many nouns used in finance are only used with a limited and predictable range of verbs. Learners should think about how they write down and store new vocabulary and be encouraged to record them in a collocation, a phrase or a sentence.

ANSWERS
1 1c 2g 3a 4b 5f 6d 7h 8e
2 1 con'glomerates   5 regu'lation
   2 de'positors   6 re'pealed
   3 de'regulated   7 'underwriting
   4 pro'hibited

NOTES

Word stress is important for comprehension (at least by native speakers); learners should be encouraged to systematically mark the stressed syllable of new words they write down.

The rules (or at least regularities) of word stress are given in a number of books, including in the 'Language reference' section of *Professional English in Use Finance* (Cambridge University Press, 2006). Most of the words in this exercise are stressed on the second syllable, as the first syllable is a prefix. The exceptions are *regulation*, because the beginning of the suffix *-ation* is regularly stressed, and *underwriting*, which is better analysed as a compound noun than as a word with a prefix.

Reading: Regulation and deregulation

Students can read the text individually first, thinking about their answers. Then they can check their answers in pairs. Finally, you can elicit answers from the whole group.

Here, and throughout the course, encourage learners to give the reasons for their true and false answers by referring to the text, or by paraphrasing it in their own words.

Discussion

If the learners do not know the answers to these questions, they could be invited to find out before the next lesson. Regulatory agencies tend to have large and informative websites, and lists of banks are also quite easy to find on the internet. The third question is more abstract, but learners working in banking may have something to say. Essentially, regulation protects the customer, but tends to limit financial institutions' room to manoeuvre. The subject of regulation reappears towards the end of the course, in **Unit 23**.

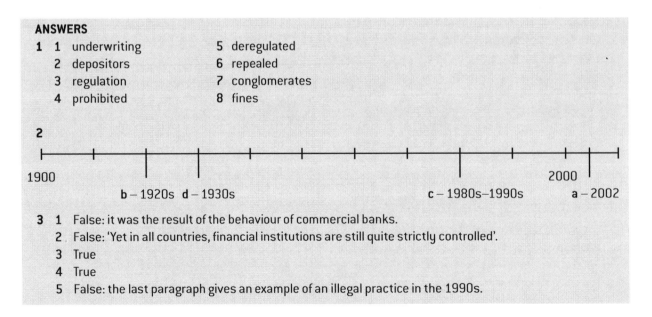

ANSWERS
1 1 underwriting   5 deregulated
   2 depositors   6 repealed
   3 regulation   7 conglomerates
   4 prohibited   8 fines

2

1900   2000

b – 1920s d – 1930s   c – 1980s–1990s   a – 2002

3 1 False: it was the result of the behaviour of commercial banks.
   2 False: 'Yet in all countries, financial institutions are still quite strictly controlled'.
   3 True
   4 True
   5 False: the last paragraph gives an example of an illegal practice in the 1990s.

Language focus: Possibility, necessity and prohibition

This section looks at ways of expressing possibility, necessity and prohibition. Before looking at the exercise, ask learners to think about regulations in their place of work or study and to give an example of things which are possible, necessary or prohibited. For example, *It is forbidden to smoke.* You could then ask them if they can think of another way of saying this. Learners with a Latin-based first language (such as Spanish, French or Italian) often tend to use *It is possible / necessary to ...* whereas native speakers usually use the modal equivalent.

Ask learners to read the sentences and make sure the first task is clear. The second task asks learners to classify the sentences according to their meaning. Work through the example to ensure learners understand what to do. They should then think about their answers individually before checking them in pairs.

ANSWERS

1
1. Although banks <u>are allowed to</u> open on Saturdays, most of them don't.
2. Banks <u>aren't allowed to</u> charge less than the minimum interest rate.
3. Commercial banks <u>have to</u> deposit part of their reserves at the central bank.
4. If you have a credit card, you <u>don't need to</u> pay cash.
5. If you keep at least $1,000 in the bank, you <u>don't have to</u> pay charges.
6. Today retail banks <u>need to</u> react to competition from building societies.
7. Our policy states that we <u>can't</u> lend you more than one month's salary.
8. You <u>can</u> pay me back at the end of the month.
9. You <u>must</u> keep at least $1,000 in the account if you want free banking.
10. You <u>mustn't</u> use this loan for any other purpose.
11. You <u>needn't</u> go to the bank – you can do it on the internet.

2

Meaning	Permission	Necessity or obligation	No necessity or no obligation	Prohibition
Sentence number	1, 8	3, 6, 9	4, 5, 11	2, 7, 10
Verbs used	be allowed to can	have to need to must	don't need to don't have to needn't	not be allowed to can't mustn't

3
1. were not allowed to / couldn't
2. can / are allowed to
3. don't have to, don't need to / needn't
4. were not allowed to / couldn't
5. mustn't / aren't allowed to / can't
6. needn't, don't need to / don't have to
7. allowed to / able to
8. were not allowed to / couldn't
9. have to, need to / must (*must* would probably come before *still*)
10. didn't have to / didn't need to

NOTE

Need is both a regular verb and a modal verb, but the modal usage (e.g. *Need banks compete with building societies?*) is rare. The regular verb is followed by an infinitive with *to* (the *to* is underlined in the answers above).

The most difficult aspects are probably the past forms of the modal verbs (or lack of them), and the use of the verbs expressing lack of obligation or necessity, especially the difference between *mustn't* and *don't*

have to. (German speakers in particular often find this difficult, as the German *müssen nicht* means 'don't have to'.)

Could and *was / were able to* are both used to talk about a past possibility. The difference is that *was able to* describes one specific action, whereas *could* describes a general past ability, e.g. *I could speak German quite well so I was able to get the job.*

Practice

See **pages 115** and **123** of the **Student's Book** for the file cards.

This role play, to be done in pairs, gives learners the chance to use the verbs from the **Language focus** to talk about the terms and conditions for different kinds of bank accounts. You could ask learners what kind of bank account they have and if they have more than one. You could ask them what the regulations or *terms and conditions* are for each (e.g. Do you have to keep a minimum balance in the account to avoid charges?) Each role has two parts, a call centre employee (explaining terms and conditions) and a customer (asking for information about a bank account).

Assign each learner a role (A or B) and ask them to read it through and make sure they understand the vocabulary. You may need to explain the terms *overdraft*, *balance*, *statement*, *transaction* and *ATM*. Ask the learners to prepare their questions and answers and encourage them to use the language from the **Language focus**.

When the learners are ready, Role A, Call 1 (the call centre employee) could begin by saying *Can I help you?* When they have completed the first call, they should move on to the second, with Role B, Call 2 starting the conversation.

Try to listen to as many of these conversations as you can, making a note of both good use of language and that which needs to be corrected, so that you can give feedback at the end of the activity. You might want to pick out two or three pairs of students to perform their dialogues in front of the rest of the class.

ADDITIONAL SPEAKING ACTIVITY

This could involve the learners asking questions about each other's job contracts – things they can do, can't do, don't have to do and mustn't do in their job (or, if they are studying, at their school or university). Examples might include working hours (Can they work evenings and weekends?), whether they have to attend training courses, whether there is a dress code specifying what they can and can't wear at work, whether they are allowed to choose when they take their holiday, etc.

2 Telephoning

To learn how to: handle information and make arrangements on the telephone

To practise: asking for and giving information and arranging meetings on the telephone

Lead in

These questions provide a possible way into the unit. Even if they spend a lot of time on their mobile or cell phone in their native language, many learners find it difficult to use the telephone in English – ask them to explain exactly what is difficult.

The cartoon from the *New Yorker* towards the end of the last millennium might provoke some discussion about the use of mobile phones ... unless your learners are the sort of people who use their phones loudly and incessantly in restaurants!

Listening 1: Arranging meetings

Many of the exercises in the even-numbered units begin with elicitation. With books closed, ask learners if they know any phrases they can use for arranging meetings on the phone. They can do this in pairs or small groups, or you could elicit answers from the whole class, writing them up as necessary.

Phrases for several of these functions appear in both dialogues. You will probably need to play each dialogue at least twice.

2.1 TAPESCRIPT

Call 1

Pat: ... I'm not sure that's possible. You know, Kim, I think we should have a meeting about this.

Kim: Sure. Are you free on Thursday?

Pat: Let me just check my diary. Sorry, I'm busy on Thursday. Is Friday OK?

Kim: Yes. How about nine o'clock?

Pat: Yes, nine o'clock is fine. Your office or mine?

Kim: Oh, I'll come to your office if you like.

Pat: OK, see you on Friday at nine in my office.

Kim: OK. See you then.

Call 2

Pat: Hello, Pat again. Something's come up. I have to go to Head Office on Friday. Can we make it next Monday instead?

Kim: No, sorry, I can't manage Monday, clients all day. Can you do Tuesday?

Pat: Sorry, Tuesday's not convenient. I'm busy non-stop. How about Wednesday?

Kim: OK, let's say eleven o'clock. Would that suit you?

Pat: Yes, that's fine, Wednesday at eleven. I'll come over to you. Sorry to mess you around like this.

Kim: No problem. I'll confirm that by email.

Pat: It's OK, I don't need an email – I'll be there. Bye.

1, 2 The phrases used in the recordings are in italics.

1 Ask for a meeting: Could we have / arrange a meeting? *I think we should have a meeting about this.*	**5** Suggest another day or time: What / How about Monday? *Is Friday OK?* *Can we make it next Monday instead?* *Can you do Tuesday?*
2 Suggest a day: Is Thursday convenient? What about Tuesday? *Are you free on Thursday?* *How about Wednesday?*	**6** Say that day or time is possible: Yes, that would be fine. *Yes, 9 o'clock is fine.* *Yes, that's fine, Wednesday at 11.*
3 Suggest a time: Would 1.30 be convenient? What about 2 o'clock? *How about 9 o'clock?* *Let's say 11 o'clock. Would that suit you?*	**7** Arrange the place: Where shall we meet? Shall we meet at my office? *Your office or mine?* *I'll come to your office if you like.* *I'll come over to you.*
4 Say that a day or time is not possible: I'm afraid I can't make Wednesday. Sorry, I'm tied up then. *Sorry, I'm busy on Thursday.* *No, sorry, I can't manage Monday.* *Sorry, Tuesday's not convenient.*	**8** Confirm the arrangement: I look forward to seeing you on Thursday at 10. *OK, see you on Friday at 9 in my office.* *I'll confirm that by email.*

3 With a couple of exceptions, these phrases have a standard level of formality, and could be used with both colleagues and customers. *Can you do Tuesday?* and *Your office or mine?* are relatively informal, and would probably not be used with people outside the company, unless you know them very well.

4 1e 2c 3d 4h 5j 6i 7b 8g 9a 10f

VOCABULARY NOTE
In American English, the word *diary* is not used in a business context, where the word *schedule* or *calendar* would be used.

Practice 1

See **pages 115, 123, 134** and **132** of the **Student's Book** for the file cards.

The names in this role play have been chosen because in Anglophone countries, Pat, Kim, Robin and Chris are unisex names.

The learners can do this in groups of four, or two or more students can prepare each role and you can choose one of them to do the role play. They should try to use some of the phrases which they have just heard / discussed in the previous exercises.

When they are ready, Role A (Kim Brown) should begin by greeting his / her colleagues and explaining the reason for the call. Make sure learners understand that they are all on the same conference telephone line. The learners need to look at their diaries for the following day and try to find a possible time for the meeting. Kim Brown should <u>not</u> take no for an answer – everyone must attend the meeting.

Language focus: Pronouncing the alphabet and saying telephone numbers

Learners need to be able to do this, as it is often necessary to spell names or give numbers on the telephone. Learners should practise the sentences several times individually or in pairs before reading them out to the class. Many learners find long numbers difficult, and may need more practice.

ANSWERS

1 My home number is oh oh four four, two oh seven, two seven oh, one two three four / double oh double four, two oh seven, two seven oh, one two three four (British English) / zero zero four four, two zero seven, two seven zero, one two three four (American English).
2 And my fax is two oh seven, nine two five, oh nine one eight / two zero seven, nine two five, zero nine one eight.
3 Call me on my mobile: oh eight seven, nine double six, three four, oh two / zero eight seven, nine double six, three four, zero two.
4 The winning lottery ticket was QY two nine nine, six six four, five three two / two double nine, double six four, five three two – and mine was QY two nine nine, six six four, five three three / two double nine, double six four, five double three.
5 His car number plate is AZ three one four, five eight six.

Listening 2: Handling information

In this exercise, learners will have practice in listening and writing down information – both names and numbers. First, ask learners to read through the form to make sure they understand the vocabulary. You may need to explain the term *secured* for a loan: in this context, it means 'guaranteed'.

You may need to play this recording more than twice to allow the learners to complete both tasks.

2.2 TAPESCRIPT

Customer: Hello, this is Mr Kolodziejczyk. I have a current account and a mortgage with you, and I'm calling for some information about loans.

Bank: Yes Mr Kolo ... , yes sir, what would you like to know?

Customer: I'd like to borrow £25,000 to buy a boat, and I'd like to know what interest rate you'd charge.

Bank: Well, our personal loans currently have a typical annual rate of six point four percent.

Customer: Six point four, yes. But could you tell me about secured loans? I read something somewhere about them being cheaper.

Bank: Yes, of course. That's right. If the loan is secured against a home, a life assurance policy or another suitable asset, the typical annual rate is only five percent. What type of security do you have in mind? Your home?

Customer: Yes, I've nearly paid off my mortgage.

Bank: That would probably be acceptable. And the loan can be for any term up to twenty years. When and how are you thinking of paying back?

Customer: Well, I'm not sure. I would probably want to repay capital and interest together each month. But it depends. Maybe I'd prefer to pay the interest only, and to repay the capital after five or six years.

Bank: OK. Perhaps it would be better if I sent you an application form for a secured loan. Could you give me your name again?

Customer: Kolodziejczyk. That's K-O-L-O-D-Z-I-E-J-C-Z-Y-K. It's Polish.

Bank: Yes, thank you. And your first name?

Customer: Stephen. Well actually it's Szczepan – S-Z-C-Z-E-P-A-N – but these days I spell it S-T-E-P-H-E-N. You have my address. I'm sure I'm the only Stephen Kolodziejczyk at your branch. But can I leave you a new mobile number? It's zero seven eight, nine one nine, double three seven two.

Useful phrases

Practice 2

See **pages 115** and **124** of the **Student's Book** for the file cards.

In this role play, learners can practise asking for and giving information over the phone. Divide the learners into pairs and assign each learner a role (A or B). Ask them to read through the information on the role card and ensure the vocabulary is clear. You may need to explain the terms *placements*, *eligible* and *pension* which appear on role card B. Give them a few minutes to prepare their role. When they are ready, Role B (Training Manager) should begin by answering the phone with *Can I help you?* The learners should be encouraged to use appropriate telephone phrases to begin and end the calls.

One pair can be chosen to perform their role play in front of the class.

ADDITIONAL SPEAKING ACTIVITY

This activity or game is often known as 'Chinese whispers'. In many other languages it is called the equivalent of 'broken telephone' or 'deaf telephone'. Tell the learners you are going to give them spoken messages which they need to pass around the class. The message should start at one point and be passed from one learner to the next until it arrives back at the starting point.

With a large class you can have several messages being communicated at the same time, in the same direction, with maybe 20-second intervals. Or have one message at a time, but starting and finishing in different places.

You can invent your own sentences with local references, or use some of the following:

We spent a lot more than we lent.
Can you turn up the heating for the meeting with Mrs Keating?
Congratulations on completing the Keating deal.
Thanks for improving the bank's ranking.
We're unique in New York.
The meeting finished around sixish.
Can you imagine managing this mess?
What is Mary's yearly salary?

This is a very good way to practise both listening and clear pronunciation. You could also dictate the sentences, for learners to write in their notebooks or up on the board, after they've been passed around.

3 Retail banking

AIMS

To learn about: developments in retail banking, banking products and services; key vocabulary of retail banking
To learn how to: express likelihood and probability
To practise: talking about the future of retail banking

BACKGROUND: RETAIL BANKING

This unit deals with the area of the financial industry of which almost everyone has some knowledge and experience, as customers: commercial or retail banking. (This is as opposed to investment banking, with which only people working in the financial departments of companies, and the banks they deal with, will have first-hand experience.) It discusses recent developments in the industry, most notably the growth of telephone and internet banking. (See also the notes to the **Lead in** below.)

Lead in

These opening questions can be discussed in pairs, or you could elicit answers from the whole class. Even if your learners are not yet working in the financial sector, they will have experience of commercial banks as customers. The first two questions are answered in **Unit 1**: retail banks receive deposits and make loans, while investment banks advise companies and raise capital for them. The third question is only explicitly answered in **Unit 5**, but learners will probably know the answer: as well as charging fees and commissions for all their services, commercial banks charge a higher rate for loans than they pay on deposits.

Reading 1: Commercial and investment banking

The extract is from *Liar's Poker* by Michael Lewis (London: Coronet, 1990) pp. 29–30. (This is, of course, Michael Lewis the American author, not Michael Lewis the English applied linguist and proponent of the lexical approach to language teaching.)

ANSWERS

1   1   Commercial bankers: Lewis caricatures commercial bankers as ordinary and rather boring people with boring suburban lives, who only obey instructions. He jokes about them lending hundreds of millions of dollars a day to South American countries because Western banks lent billions of dollars to Latin American governments in the 1980s, in loans that the borrowers later defaulted on. But, he says, the average commercial banker 'meant no harm' and was 'only doing what he was told'.

     2   Investment bankers: He caricatures investment bankers as brilliant, ambitious, aggressive troublemakers.

2   1   to strip out
     2   reputed to be
     3   meant no harm
     4   an endless chain of command
     5   a breed apart
     6   vast

3   'Most people' do not become investment bankers, though perhaps most people working in banking do. No commercial banker ever lent a few hundred million dollars to South American countries 'every day'. It is impossible to have 2.2 children, even if this is a statistical average. Investment bankers may possess vast, almost unimaginable, ambition – but not necessarily talent. Most investment bankers would probably be happy with only two little red sports cars!

Discussion

Depending on the type of learners you have, this question could be opened up to the whole class. If your learners are pre-work, they might have strong ideas about what area of finance they want to work in. If they are already working, you could ask them why they chose that particular field. Either way, they should have the opportunity to give their opinions about the text above.

Vocabulary 1

This short exercise is designed to make the subsequent **Listening** activity easier. If your learners are already working in the finance sector, these terms may be familiar. If not, they may know some of them. Learners could complete the matching activity individually first and then check their answers in pairs. If you have a mixed group of pre- and in-service learners, you can use the in-service learners to help explain some of the unknown terms to their less-experienced colleagues. (Using English, of course!)

> **ANSWERS**
> | | | | |
> |---|---|---|---|
> | 1 | trend | 5 | lucrative |
> | 2 | income | 6 | national income |
> | 3 | assets | 7 | currency |
> | 4 | liabilities | | |

NOTE

With learners who do not know accounting terminology in English (covered later in **Unit 7**), it might be helpful to talk about *assets* and *liabilities* in more detail (the terms are also defined in **Unit 7**). It is important to understand that a *bank's* assets are the money that it has loaned to customers and its liabilities are the money that its customers have deposited. This is, in a sense, the contrary of other businesses: for most businesses, money deposited in a bank is an asset, and a loan is a liability.

Listening: Retail banking

Learners can listen the first time and answer Question 1 to get the gist of the script. Then ask them to read through the true / false task to make sure it is clear. The vocabulary has been defined in the **Vocabulary** exercise. Learners can complete the task individually, then listen again and check their answers in pairs. Ask the learners to give reasons for their choice of true or false.

3 TAPESCRIPT

Peter Sinclair: Well, I'm not sure that retail banking is declining. I think in many countries the size of bank deposits, that's the liabilities that the retail banks have, has been growing faster than national income – it's been rising. People are increasingly moving away from currency towards things like bank deposits, that's a slow gradual trend and it's a trend evident in most places, especially the more developing poorer countries, emerging economies and so on.

So I think retail banking has always been regarded as important, but perhaps a little boring for some people. So the real action seems to be more in the big-scale operations with large companies, in huge deals and other kinds of activity which are thought to be more sophisticated and perhaps more rewarding than retail banking. More sophisticated yes, more specialized yes, but not more lucrative, and often more dangerous. Retail banking I think is not in decline; although people have been predicting that it might be at some point, there's no evidence that it is.

> **ANSWERS**
>
> 1 Peter Sinclair says that there is no evidence that retail banking is in decline.
>
> 2 1 True: 'People are increasingly moving away from currency towards things like bank deposits.'
>
>   2 False: Sinclair says that the volume of bank deposits has been growing faster than national income.
>
>   3 True: 'So the real action seems to be more in the big-scale operations with large companies, in huge deals ...'.
>
>   4 False: '... but not more lucrative'.
>
>   5 True: '... often more dangerous'.

Discussion

These questions can be discussed briefly, in pairs, small groups, or with the whole class. Major developments in retail banking include telephone banking and e-banking. These developments, and possible future trends, are considered in the following activities.

Vocabulary 2

These are basic terms in retail banking, known to most customers with bank accounts. Some of these will have come up in the **Practice** activity in **Unit 1**.

> **ANSWERS**
>
> **1** 1 direct debit
> 2 savings account
> 3 statement
> 4 overdraft
> 5 current account
> 6 loan
> 7 balance
> 8 standing order
>
> **2** Common word combinations include:
> apply for a loan
> apply for an overdraft
> cancel a cheque
> cancel a direct debit
> cancel a standing order
> check the balance
> set up a direct debit
> set up a standing order
> transfer money
> write a cheque
>
> Other combinations are also possible, such as *transfer the balance* (when you close an account) and *check an overdraft* (to see if you've spent too much).

VOCABULARY NOTES

This web page is written in British English. In American English, *cheque* is spelt *check*, and there is only one *l* in *traveller*. American English would also use *lining up* or *standing in line* rather than *queuing*.

Reading 2: The future of bank branches

The article is from the *Financial Times*, 18 September 2002. It is easier to read than the excerpt from Michael Lewis earlier in the unit. Ask learners to look first at the headline and predict what the text could be about. Then ask them to read the text quickly and find the answer to the first question (you could set a time limit of 1–2 minutes depending on your learners).

Once you have discussed the first answer and the learners have a general idea about the content of the article, they can do the second task. Again, they can complete this individually first, before comparing their answers in pairs.

Finally, they should be able to answer the questions in Task 3 and complete the pie chart in 4.

VOCABULARY NOTE

The third paragraph uses *bank* as a verb.

> **ANSWERS**
>
> **1** It shows that it is not true that more affluent and sophisticated customers prefer not to use bank branches.
>
> **2** 1 drive future growth
> 2 affluent
> 3 a decade of under-investment
> 4 ahead of the game
> 5 invest substantially
> 6 reshaping
> 7 staffing
>
> **3** 1 They have not invested enough in their branches.
> 2 They are expected to concentrate more on their branches than on telephone and internet banking, and offer new services in them.
> 3 The bank (Abbey National) has introduced coffee shops into some branches.
>
> **4**
>
>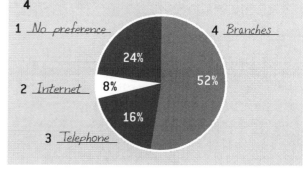
>
> 1 *No preference*
> 2 *Internet*
> 3 *Telephone*
> 4 *Branches*
> 24% 8% 52% 16%

Discussion

The advantages of internet banking for the customer include time flexibility: you can do your banking any time you are connected to the internet. Similarly with telephone banking: if the bank's phone lines are open 24 hours a day, you can do your banking whenever you like. Cash points or ATMs are convenient for withdrawing, and sometimes depositing, cash. Electronic payment methods avoid the need to use cash. On the other hand, branches offer personal contact, and telephone and e-banking raise some security issues: are passwords and data safe? Branches are clearly more convenient if they are well situated, open longer hours, and efficient, i.e. if they have enough staff to prevent customers having to queue for a long time.

People who are at work during bank opening hours are likely to prefer electronic banking. Older and retired people often have the time to go to bank branches, and prefer the personal contact they get there to the anonymous contact of electronic banking. Poorer people are unlikely to have free access to the telephone and internet. As there are customers who prefer each of the three delivery channels, banks are more or less obliged to provide all the options.

Internet and telephone banking allow reductions in the costs of retail and office space (the bank's premises), but involve extra costs in IT staff. Call centres (or Customer Service Centres) for answering telephone calls to Anglophone banks are increasingly being outsourced to foreign countries (such as India) where salaries are lower.

Banks usually find face-to-face contact with customers more effective for achieving sales of banking products. Relationship management and retaining loyal customers are made easier by having counselling areas with financial advisors in bank branches.

Language focus: Likelihood and probability

In this exercise, learners have to decide the level of probability expressed in the example sentences. Ask the learners to read through the sentences and make sure they understand them. They may not know phrases like *be bound to* or *are likely to* so you may need to explain them. Learners could try to match the sentences to the scale individually first before checking their answers in pairs or small groups. To vary this pattern, you could ask learners to work together in pairs first before checking the answers with the whole group.

ANSWERS

1

1	certain (100%)	e	Our profits will definitely increase this year.
		g	Small regional banks are bound to join together.
2	probable (>70%)	b	I may well decide to change banks.
		h	They'll probably move their call centre to India.
		i	Universal banks are likely to spread.
		k	We expect all banks to invest substantially in their branch networks.
3	possible (≈50%)	f	Perhaps we need to hire more financial advisors.
		l	We might increase our commission charges.
4	improbable (<30%)	a	E-banking is unlikely to decrease over the next 10 years.
		d	There could be a takeover, but I think it's improbable.
5	impossible (0%)	c	Interest rates can't possibly stay so low.
		j	We certainly won't reduce the size of our counselling area.

2 Other common ways of expressing probability include:

certain (100%)	will definitely / will certainly / is certain to / is sure to / must / has to
probable (>70%)	It is (very / highly / extremely) probable / likely that ...
possible (≈50%)	It is possible that ... will possibly / maybe / may / could
improbable (<30%)	It is (very / highly / extremely) unlikely that ...
impossible (0%)	There's no way that ... definitely will not (won't) / can't possibly

NOTE

The examples given largely concern the future, although one can, of course, also refer to the likelihood of present and past events: *Perhaps she's on the train*, *He probably didn't mean that*, etc.

Discussion

The aim of this exercise is to give learners practice with the phrases introduced in the **Language focus** above. You could give learners two or three topics each to think about and prepare a few predictions. They could then talk about these in pairs or small groups. Alternatively, you could open this up as a 'free' discussion, allowing all the learners the chance to give their predictions about each of the topics.

Practice

See **pages 115**, **124** and **134** of the **Student's Book** for the file cards.

The aim of this activity is to give learners further practice in the language and vocabulary introduced in this unit. Divide the learners into groups of three and assign each learner a role. Learners may need 15–20 minutes (or more, depending on their language level and level of confidence) to prepare their roles. Only three people are needed for the meeting itself, though each of the heads of department could be accompanied by an assistant. Learners should be encouraged to use some of the phrases from the **Language focus**.

The Chief Operating Officer has called the meeting and should therefore act as chair, encouraging both sides to give their opinions and to reach a final decision which will be presented to the Board. You could help the learner with this role by giving some phrases that could be used for asking for / giving opinions, starting and finishing the meeting (see **Units 10** and **12** for examples).

The Head of Retail Operations will presumably cite the research reported in the *Financial Times* article. He or she should be encouraged to provide specific, concrete suggestions as to what could be done in the branches (some examples are provided on the role card).

The Head of Internet Banking could attempt to dismiss the research findings and argue for the inevitable growth of the internet, or attack the costs involved in relocating, refurbishing or redesigning bank branches.

The result of the meeting is unpredictable, and will depend either on the persuasiveness of the learners taking the Head of Retail Operations and Head of Internet Banking roles, or on the preconceived notions of the learner taking the Chief Operating Officer role! After the role play, the class can discuss whether they agree with the decision taken at the meeting.

4 Business correspondence 1

To learn how to: write emails using standard phrases; use formal and informal style

To practise: writing business emails; saying email and web addresses

Lead in

These questions are designed as a way in to the topic. Even if your learners do not work in business yet, they probably use email and may have ideas about its advantages and disadvantages. When discussing this topic, it is worth reminding learners that native speakers often telephone if they want to discuss something and send an email to confirm. This is because written communication is seen as more 'fixed'. People working in foreign languages in which they are not entirely confident sometimes prefer to use emails when they want to discuss something and only use the phone as a last resort.

Discussion

You can expect most learners to agree with most of these statements, perhaps with the following exceptions.

ANSWERS

4 Some people might say that emails are more informal and may have examples of first emails which use first names, but it is probably better for learners to use the 'safer', more formal option.

5 It depends on the length of the thread, and you certainly shouldn't reply at the bottom of a lengthy thread.

6 It is not always possible to keep messages this short, and the part about mobile devices is almost certainly an overgeneralization.

8 Some things are clearer in writing.

15 This probably depends on who you are writing to, and what the business is.

16 This is deliberately misspelled!

Language focus: Formal and informal style 1

ANSWERS

1 When people write emails <u>to</u> friends they often use a <u>very</u> informal style. <u>They</u> <u>don't</u> worry much about <u>spelling</u>, using capital letters<u>,</u> using correct <u>grammar</u>, writing in paragraphs, punctuation and so on. <u>Sometimes they use <u>abbreviations</u> like in <u>text</u> messages. <u>You</u> definitely <u>shouldn't</u> do this when writing <u>business</u> emails.

2 1c 2a 3e 4b 5f 6d

3 1d 2a 3c 4d 5b 6e 7b 8a/e 9c 10a

Writing 1

ANSWERS

1 1j 2a 3b 4g 5h 6f 7i 8e 9c 10d

2 1 reserved   2 receive   3 request
   4 require   5 inform

POSSIBLE ANSWERS

3

> Hi Steve
>
> <u>The</u> meeting went well. <u>It's a</u> pity you couldn't be there. <u>We / We've</u> decided to invest up to £5m on 3 new branches in shopping centres. <u>They</u> will have large open counselling areas <u>(and)</u> that sort of thing, <u>(and)</u> not just counters. <u>I</u> hope that makes you happy! <u>We / I</u> will start looking for suitable premises <u>as soon as possible</u>. Using <u>an</u> agency <u>is</u> probably <u>(would</u> probably <u>be)</u> quicker. Maybe TCP – <u>I</u> think it means Town Centre Properties. <u>Have you</u> ever worked with them?
>
> <u>I'll</u> talk to you tomorrow.
>
> Sonia

4

> Dear all
>
> This is just to summarize the key points from our meeting.
>
> - We decided to organize a survey to <u>look into</u> our customers' opinions about our services.
> - Susan will <u>give</u> a brief to the marketing team.
> - John will contact the finance department to <u>get</u> the funding so that we can <u>begin</u> as soon as possible.
> - I will <u>make sure</u> that the staff in the branches are <u>told</u>.
>
> <u>Feel free</u> to contact me if you want to discuss or <u>check</u> any of these points.
>
> Kind regards
>
> David

NOTE

As this is a more informal email, the Latin-based words have been replaced with shorter, 'Anglo-Saxon' equivalents or phrasal verbs.

Useful phrases

ANSWERS

1 Get back to me if there are any problems.
2 I look forward to seeing you next week.
3 I'm sending the report as an attachment.
4 Let me know if there's anything I can do.
5 Please complete the attached form and return it asap.
6 Thanks in advance for your help in this matter.
7 This is just to confirm our phone call.
8 Sorry, I forgot to add the attachment!

Vocabulary

ANSWERS

1	dot	6	underscore
2	colon	7	upper case
3	lower case	8	small letter
4	capital letter	9	dash
5	slash	10	at

Practice

See **pages 116** and **124** of the **Student's Book** for the file cards.

As with other role plays, give the learners time to prepare their role. If you want to make this more challenging / realistic, you could ask learners to sit back-to-back so that they cannot see their partner's information and it is more like a real phone call. However, if you have a large class, this can be very noisy. If possible, have the learners try to access the addresses they write down, to see whether they are correct (provided the sites still exist).

VOCABULARY NOTE

Some learners may prefer the term *URL* to web address. It stands for Uniform Resource Locator.

Writing 2

POSSIBLE ANSWER

> Date:
> From: Kim Brown
> To: Robin.Black@ ..., Pat.Green@ ...,
>   Chris.White@ ...
> Cc: Jean.Chance@ ...
> Subject: Tomorrow's meeting with Jean Chance
>
> Dear all
>
> This is to confirm that you are meeting Mrs Chance in her office at 8.30 tomorrow morning.
>
> The meeting should last about an hour.
>
> Kind regards
>
> Kim Brown
>
> Assistant to the Risk Manager

VOCABULARY NOTE

The phrase *meeting with* (instead of just *meeting*) is becoming increasingly popular, especially in American English.

ADDITIONAL WRITING ACTIVITIES

The conference call in **Unit 2** could easily give rise to several further emails: for example, Robin Black asking someone else to pick up his / her tickets at the travel agents, and rearranging the meeting with Chris White; Pat Green rearranging the introductory talk for the trainees and the scheduled meeting with the Chief Executive; and perhaps Chris White warning that he / she might have to interview the financial accounting candidate a bit later.

BACKGROUND: LOANS AND CREDIT

5 Loans and credit

AIMS

To learn about: lending decisions; key vocabulary of loans and credit
To learn how to: give advice and make suggestions
To practise: making lending decisions; giving advice to clients

The interest rate at which a company is able to borrow largely depends on its credit standing, as established by ratings companies and estimated by the research departments of investment banks. Investors usually expect a premium (a higher interest rate, or *yield*, or *coupon*) for greater risk. Bonds issued by companies with a bad credit rating are commonly known as *junk bonds*. Some investors buy these as they are prepared to take the risk of default (non-repayment of the principal at maturity) in return for a higher interest rate.

Bonds are also issued by national and local governments. Government bonds, which can last up to thirty years or more, are known as *treasury bonds* in the USA and *gilt-edged stock* or just *gilts* in Britain. These are generally considered to be the safest form of investment. In some countries, central banks also issue short-term bonds, called *treasury bills*, in order to regulate the money supply and influence interest rates.

Corporate bonds are generally considered to be safer than investments in stocks, though a company's financial situation can change during the life of a bond, which is usually between five and ten years. Bondholders generally receive fixed interest payments, though there are also *floating-rate bonds*, as well as *zero coupon bonds* that pay no interest but are sold at a discount to their *par value* (also called *nominal* or *face value* – the value which is written on the bond).

Bonds are traded by banks which act as market makers on behalf of their customers. Bond traders make a market with two prices: a *bid price* at which they buy and an *offer price* at which they sell. The difference (or *spread*) between these two prices is generally very small, but traders can sell enormous quantities of bonds in a single day, which can be another significant source of income for banks.

The price of bonds fluctuates inversely with interest rates. If interest rates increase, so that new borrowers have to pay a higher rate, existing bonds lose value. On the contrary, if interest rates fall, existing bonds paying a higher interest rate than the market rate will logically increase in value. Consequently the yield of a bond bought on the secondary market depends on its purchase price as well as its interest rate.

Smaller and less well-known companies do not have the possibility of issuing bonds, and so are often dependent on bank loans if they need to borrow.

Lead in

Learners working in finance should be able to answer these questions. The first three are more or less answered in the **Listening** section.

ANSWERS

- By charging higher interest rates to borrowers than they pay to depositors.
- By assessing the potential borrower's creditworthiness.
- Essentially, by calculating the risk that the loan will not be repaid.
- As mentioned in the definition of corporate bonds from www.finance-glossary.com, companies either borrow money in the form of loans or bonds (debt finance), or issue stocks or shares (equity finance). Equity is not borrowing, because the capital does not have to be paid back: the stocks or shares represent part-ownership of the company (see **Unit 15**).
- Because they are able to issue bonds (to institutional investors and the general public) at a lower cost (interest rate) than a bank loan.

Reading: Banks and bonds

Vocabulary

Learners can be expected to know some, if not all, of these words. They should certainly be able to deduce EBIT! You could ask learners to do this exercise in pairs initially and then check the answers with the whole class.

5.1 = TRACK 7
5.2 = 8

Listening 1: Lending decisions

As usual, learners can listen once, and then a second time to check or complete their answers. Most of the words required are in the preceding **Vocabulary** exercise.

5.1 TAPESCRIPT

Interviewer: How do banks decide who to lend to?

Gerlinde Igler: Normally we analyse the customers. That means that we analyse the annual reports, the figures during the year. We have to analyse how the company will develop in the future. So we evaluate the current situation of the customer and the future situation of the customer.

We also discuss the loan with the customers – what kind of loan is it? Is it a short-term loan or is it a long-term loan? It's very important to know the maturity of this loan. If we lend money for a long time we have to be sure that the customer can repay this loan. Normally the company must be able to repay the loan from the operating cash flow, the EBIT of the company.

Our decision also depends on the bank's portfolio. We finance different sectors in industry, and we've got different limits for the sectors. And if we overstep this limit with the new customer, we need a new approval for the higher limit for the sector, and we have to decide if it's OK to increase the credit limit for the sector.

We also have a rating for each sector, and we have to decide if it is a sector with a good rating or a sector with a bad rating. If you have a sector with a bad rating we normally only finance the best companies in this sector.

Sometimes the customer would like to finance some different transactions in foreign countries. If we finance transactions in Eastern Europe or in Asia we have to look at the country rating and we have to look at the limit for this country. For these countries we have limits or we have no limits. If we don't have a limit for this country we can't finance it – it's too dangerous.

NOTE

In this interview, Gerlinde Igler is only talking about lending to <u>corporate</u> customers. There is a different credit assessment process for personal lending, which relies almost entirely on automated credit scoring systems. These calculate the customer's ability to repay (monthly income less expenditure), to which the bank can, if it wishes, add a specific judgement on the customer's willingness to repay, which will involve looking at their credit history, stability, financial security, and so on.

Listening 2: Margins

5.2 TAPESCRIPT

Gerlinde Igler: The last important point is that we would like to earn money with the customer [laughs]; we need an agreement about the margin. We have a special system, a special calculation system, in which we calculate the margin, and the margin is added to the cost of funds, and the cost of funds plus the margin is then the interest rate of the customers. We need an acceptable margin.

The cost of funds will depend on the market situation and the bank's rating. If you have a good rating you can get money on the capital markets more cheaply than a bank with a bad rating. Every bank is rated by the international agencies, Standard & Poor's and Moody's. It's

a big disadvantage if you don't have a Triple A rating. You have to pay higher interest for the money you borrow.

We calculate a margin and the margin includes the product costs. The product costs depend on the product the customer will use. Then we have the overhead costs. Overhead costs depend on the situation of the bank. A smaller bank has a lot of overhead costs and a big bank normally has lower overhead costs.

The most important point is the risk costs, because the risk costs depend on the customer's rating. If I have a bad customer and the customer has a bad rating, in this case the customer has to pay a higher margin. If we can get securities or collateral we can reduce our risks, because we can use this collateral if the company goes bust.

But there is a lot of competition between the banks and it's very hard for small banks to get good customers or to get acceptable margins.

Language focus: Advising and suggesting

The first activity here would be best done with books closed as some suggested answers immediately follow the question. Ask learners how they would give advice or suggestions in English. This does not have to be in a business context initially: if your class is mainly pre-service learners, it may give them confidence to realize that some of the phrases they already know can transfer to business situations.

ANSWERS

2 *How about ...*, *Have you considered ...* and *It'd be a good idea to ...* are fairly informal and could be used with a colleague; *I think you should / ought to ...* are quite forceful – *ought to* is more formal than *should*. *I'd advise you (not) to ...* and *It's advisable to ...* are fairly formal and probably only used in written English.

3 There are several possible constructions with *suggest*, *recommend* and *advise*. Learners may not come up with all of them, but it is important to make them aware that these phrases must be used as shown: i.e. followed by an infinitive or by a gerund, or by either, depending on the construction.

Phrase	Example
Could / May I suggest (that) you *do* ... I suggest *doing* ... I suggest that you *do* ... I'd (I would) recommend (that) you *do* ... I'd (I would) recommend *doing* ... I recommend that you *do* ... I'd (I would) advise you (not) *to do* ... I'd (I would) advise against *doing* ...	May I suggest you open a savings account? I suggest buying government bonds. I suggest that you pay off that debt first. I'd recommend you buy a house. I'd recommend taking insurance on this loan. I recommend that you talk to an accountant. I'd advise you (not) to sell those securities. I'd advise against borrowing so much.

4 There are no 'right answers', but typical advice would probably involve the following suggestions. Any of the phrases listed in this section could be used to begin the sentences.
1 ... withdraw (withdrawing) $3,000 from your deposit account and pay (paying) off your credit card debt.
2 ... open (opening) a higher interest savings account.
3 ... diversify (diversifying) your investments, and buy (buying) stocks in several different companies, and perhaps some bonds as well.
4 ... get (getting) a new mortgage instead, which will be cheaper than a loan.
5 ... think (thinking) about a pension plan, and start (starting) saving regular amounts of money each month.
6 ... use (using) a credit or debit card, or buy (buying) some traveller's cheques instead.
7 ... use (using) our ATMs or cash dispensers and our online banking facilities.
8 ... use (using) our night safe or our automated deposit machine instead of taking the money home.

Practice 1

See **pages 116**, **125**, **132** and **134** of the **Student's Book** for the file cards.

This activity asks learners to consider bank loan applications: the applications are from small and large companies and also from individuals. You could ask learners to remember what criteria Gerlinde Igler mentioned were important for the bank when deciding who to lend to. The aim of this activity is to give learners a chance to practise some of the vocabulary and phrases introduced in the unit. Clearly, not all learners will be involved in making these kinds of decisions

and they can use this as an opportunity to discuss and defend their point of view in a financial context.

Divide the learners into groups of 4, assigning each member of the group a role. Give learners time to read through their information and prepare their role. Each role has two cases to consider and there are eight different cases altogether. Once prepared, each group should discuss all the cases and decide whether the bank should give the loan or not. They should then rank the loans, putting them in order of priority based on how well they meet the criteria.

After the groups have made their lists you could have a whole class meeting to see which loans the groups have accepted and with which priority. Then individual learners could explain the reasons for their choices or give reasons for disagreeing with the majority choice.

Dollar amounts are used as this is an international currency. You could adapt the currency and the amounts given.

VOCABULARY NOTE

The following words occur in the cases and may need explanation:
inadequate – Case 1, *garage mechanics* – Case 2, *syndicate* – Case 3, *syndicate, toll* – Case 4, *franchise fee* – Case 5, *abandoned* – Case 6, *sponsors* – Case 7.

Practice 2

See **pages 117-8** and **125-6** of the **Student's Book** for the file cards.

This activity involves two meetings for each pair of students. Learners either have the role of customer or bank employee for the first meeting and then they take the other role for the second meeting. As customer, they have been granted a loan and are now being offered some other services by the bank. They need to listen and ask questions. As bank employee, they need to recommend some other services to the customer.

A web page with a list of the bank's services is included on the role cards. The customers in both cases (2, 5) are already asking for fixed-term loans, so would not need to discuss this service. In addition, they are both start-ups so they will probably not be interested in Executive Life Insurance.

VOCABULARY NOTE

This web page uses American English – *checks, federal taxes* and *state taxes*.

Writing

This is just a brief email to the training manager, confirming what was decided at the meeting. The content will depend on which loans were agreed.

POSSIBLE ANSWER

Dear ...

I'm writing to inform you about the decisions that were made in this morning's training exercise.

We decided to grant loans in the following cases:

- Case 5: the two graduates have good training in restaurant management and the franchise they want to open is well known and has a good support structure. The graduates have a clear business plan for repayment within two years.
  ...

Please let me know if you need any more information.

6 Business correspondence 2

Lead in

Learners could be invited in advance to bring in some examples of standard professional letters, if confidentiality permits, or examples of letters they have received as customers from their bank, insurance company, etc.

Companies tend to write letters when correspondence needs to be filed and retained for future use. If your learners are still full-time students, you could ask them about the types of formal letters they receive in everyday life. What learners find difficult about writing business letters in English probably includes their content, form, style and level of formality!

Most organizations have templates of standard letters for all common situations: a text with standard information, with spaces or blanks to be filled in, depending on the exact situation. This saves time, allows the organization to control the quality of what goes out to customers and business partners, and helps ensure compliance with regulatory, legal and organizational constraints and obligations.

This unit concentrates on letters responding to complaints because the situations are often unpredictable and not catered for by standard templates. Although they may well include formulaic phrases, replies to complaints are often unique, and consequently more difficult to write than many other forms of business correspondence.

Language focus: Formal and informal style 2

This exercise is designed to promote discussion on style – some of these situations will be somewhere in between formal and informal and you could mention this to your learners.

ANSWERS

1 1 Probably 'semi-formal'; with an old customer you don't want to be too formal, but a summary of decisions taken at a meeting will be filed for future reference.
   2 Formal
   3 Probably 'semi-formal' especially if the letter will be seen by other people.
   4 Formal
   5 Less formal, although the contract itself would be in a very formal and legal style.
   6 Formal
   7 Informal, unless the writer's fault was very great.
   8 It would depend on the company culture, but probably informal.

2 As with similar exercises (with books closed), ask the learners if they can think of any phrases for these situations. Even if they are not yet working, they will probably still have some experience of writing letters – both formal and informal.

3 1 b, c, m, n   5 d, e, f, i, j
   2 d, e, f, h   6 d, k
   3 d   7 a, g, l
   4 h

Listening 1: A letter of complaint

Ask learners to look first at the headlines and make sure they know what *credit card fraud* is. You could briefly discuss the problems of fraud and ask if learners have had any experience of this. Play the conversation once and ask learners to decide which of the statements are true. Learners will need to listen to the conversation more than once to do the second task.

⊘ 6.1 TAPESCRIPT

John: Hello?

Charlotte: Hi John, Charlotte here. I've got a very aggressive letter here I've got to answer, and I'd like a second opinion.

John: OK ...

Charlotte: We have a customer whose card was being used fraudulently, until it reached the credit limit. And she was on holiday on a small Hawaiian island and suddenly found her card didn't work, and didn't have any other way of getting cash.

John: And we didn't notice anything until too late?

Charlotte: Well, we did. It's someone ordering things from the internet, to be sent to an address in the States. We've now notified the authorities there and blocked the account. But this happened last year, and the transactions weren't fraudulent. At the time, we contacted the customer and she wrote an angry letter saying, 'Can't I buy presents for friends in America without getting stupid letters from my credit card company?' or something like that. This time, we noticed the transactions but didn't immediately do anything. So suddenly she was on the other side of the world with no money, and she couldn't pay the hotel, and she couldn't get to the airport, and she missed her flight, and so on, and she says it's all our fault.

John: And she didn't have any other cards?

Charlotte: Apparently not, and it took two days for her bank to transfer money to her. It was the weekend, there's a ten-hour time difference, she couldn't call her bank at night, and so on.

John: Well, that's unfortunate. But we explain the situation, and tell her that we would have taken action sooner over suspected fraudulent transactions if she hadn't replied to us like

that last year. Besides, if a card is being used fraudulently we have to block it, so she'd have been in the same situation anyway.

Charlotte: True, but the thing is the customer in question is the daughter of the Chairman of MGS Bank. She makes quite sure she tells us that in her letter.

John: [laughs] And he couldn't get money to her for two days?

Charlotte: Apparently not to Hawaii.

John: What about her MGS Bank debit card?

Charlotte: I think she'd reached her limit on that.

John: Well, that's not our fault, is it? Adapt the standard letter, you know, regretting the inconvenience, say we're doing everything we can to prevent fraud, etc., but absolutely not admitting liability. Show it to me before you send it, if you like.

Charlotte: OK, thanks.

ANSWERS

1 1 False   3 False
   2 True   4 True

2 1 b, d, g, c, f, e, a
   2 The answer here is a tentative 'no', given the customer's behaviour on the previous occasion that fraudulent use of the card was suspected. Moreover, as the **Listening** activity makes clear, if they had established fraudulent use they would have had to cancel the card immediately, temporarily leaving the customer in an identical situation.
   3 The answer here is equally 'no': all the company's correspondence should be courteous and polite, with the identity of the customer making no difference.

Writing 1: Replying to a letter of complaint

This situation is based on a true event. The person in question now travels with more than one method of payment!

The sentences in the letter below show typical phrases for these situations. They are numbered according to the functions listed in Question 1.

Having written example sentences, learners should find it easier to write the complete letter. This could be done individually or in pairs. They should also refer to the **Useful phrases** below.

It is always useful for learners to look at what their colleagues have written as they can learn a lot from each other, particularly if you have a class with mixed backgrounds from different areas of business or studies.

POSSIBLE ANSWERS
1, 2

Dear Ms Roberts
We are very sorry to learn about the inconvenience you suffered during your holiday in Hawaii (1), and we greatly regret the fact that your credit card details have been used fraudulently (2). At MGS Credit Cards we use the latest technology and do everything possible to prevent the fraudulent use of our customers' cards. Unfortunately, despite all our security procedures, it is impossible to completely eliminate credit card fraud (3).
Your old card has now been blocked, and we have contacted the authorities (4). Please be assured that we are continuing to investigate this matter fully (5).
A new card, with a new number, has been posted to you. You should also shortly receive, under separate cover, your PIN number (6). If you do not receive these in the next two business days, please contact us. We wish to inform you that our standard security procedures did alert us to what we thought might be unauthorized transactions using your card details. However, because of your response when we phoned you in similar circumstances last year, we did not immediately contact you (7).
Furthermore, if we had blocked your card, on suspicion that your card details were being used fraudulently, the result would have been the same: you would have been on holiday without the possibility of using your MGS Card (8). Unfortunately there is always the possibility of credit card fraud. For your future travels it would be advisable to have available an alternative means of paying bills and withdrawing cash (9). We would once again like to express our regret at the inconvenience you have been caused, and hope you will continue to use our card and benefit from all the advantages it brings (10).
Yours sincerely,

Listening 2: An angry phone call

Something similar to this also happened to someone I know. Night safes require keys, and he went to the wrong bank and found that his key wouldn't work. At that moment, someone else came along with a bag to deposit, so he took advantage of this to drop his bag in too. The next morning he got <u>four</u> police officers and <u>two</u> cars, one at the back of the house in case he tried to run away!

🔘 6.2 TAPESCRIPT

Customer: Is that MGS Bank? My name's Hewson and I work at Green's, the garden centre. The police just came round to my house, on my day off, and I was nearly arrested! And it's all your fault, because you haven't got a night safe. I want to speak to the branch manager. Now!

Bank employee: I'm sorry, Mr Hewson, I can't put you through to the manager at the moment. You'll have to explain the situation to me.

Customer: I just did! There were two policemen at my house! Accusing me!

Bank employee: Mr Hewson, if you could just try to calm down a little and explain the situation to me. I'm not quite sure I follow you.

Customer: I told you, it's your night safe. You can't use it. It's boarded over, because they're renovating the building. So I couldn't put the money in it yesterday afternoon.

Bank employee: Yes, Mr Hewson, we are renovating the building, and work has been going on for three weeks now. And we notified all our customers about this a long time ago. Now perhaps you could explain exactly what the problem is? Did you take some money home instead of depositing it?

Customer: Yes, I already told you I couldn't deposit it.

Bank employee: And this morning your manager checked the account, and the money wasn't there?

Customer: Yes.

Bank employee: And he notified the police?

Customer: Yes.

Bank employee: He didn't call you first?

Customer: I don't know, my phone wasn't turned on. I told you, it's my day off.

Bank employee: But you have the money?

Customer: Yes.

Bank employee: And you've explained this to the police? And your manager?

Customer: Yes, but I don't like being woken up by the police accusing me of stealing fifteen hundred pounds because you don't have a night safe.

Bank employee: Well, it's true that we don't have a night safe at present, but we do have an automated deposit machine in the self-service area of all our branches, next to the cash dispensers, where you can deposit both notes and coins, 24 hours a day. Are you sure your manager told you to use the night safe?

Customer: Er, I don't know. But I still want to speak to the manager! Immediately!

ANSWERS

1 The customer has attempted to use an out-of-service night safe, and then taken money home with him. Because the cash has not been deposited, his employer has informed the police who come to the customer's home the next morning.

2 This is the customer's fault: the bank has informed customers of the unavailability of the night safe, there is an automated deposit machine inside the bank, and it is unlikely that the customer's employer asked him to use the night safe.

Writing 2

Again, learners can try this exercise individually or in pairs before comparing with the rest of the class.

POSSIBLE ANSWER

Dear Mr Hewson

I refer to your phone call to the bank earlier today.

I am very sorry to learn about your unpleasant experience this morning.

However, I must inform you that we wrote to all business customers about our renovation work several weeks before it started, explaining that the night safe facility would be unavailable for two months. We also offered all our customers a key to the night safe at another branch, in case they wished to continue using this service.

We also drew our customers' attention to the automated deposit machine in the self-service area of all our branches, which is open 24 hours a day, and can be used to deposit notes and coins. I would also like to mention that Green's Garden Centre has made use of this deposit facility several times since renovation work began and the night safe was closed.

I would like, once again, to express my deepest regret for the inconvenience you experienced, and hope you will continue to benefit from the improved services our fully renovated branch will soon be offering.

Yours sincerely

Writing 3

This is one of the companies in **Unit 5, Practice 1**. Your learners may well have decided to grant the loan, which just goes to show that they know more than MGS Bank! The services advertised were in **Unit 5, Practice 2**.

ANSWERS

1 The only phrase in the **Useful phrases** that clearly accepts responsibility is *This was an error on our part*. However, *We do everything possible to ...*, and *Despite all our security procedures ...* could lead to an acceptance of responsibility. Some other phrases for admitting responsibility are:

This was our mistake ...
We are sorry for our error ...
Unfortunately, we made a mistake ...
Regrettably, this was our responsibility ...

2 **POSSIBLE ANSWER**

> Dear Mrs Strutt
>
> I refer to your letter of 4 December 20--.
>
> I am sorry we recently sent you a mailing describing you as a 'valued business customer', when in fact you currently do no business with us. This was an error on our part. Please accept our apologies.
>
> However, we still look forward to the possibility of doing business with you in the future.
>
> Yours sincerely

NOTE

The letter in the **Student's Book** has a standard layout. English-language conventions for addresses, dates, etc., differ from those of many other languages, and need to be learned. A useful way of emphasizing that we write the receiver's address on the left is to show the learners an envelope with the window on the left. (This is not always easy to find in non English-speaking countries, and unfortunately not included free with this Teacher's Book!)

7 Accounting

AIMS

To learn about: types of accounting; financial statements; key vocabulary of financial statements and accounting
To learn how to: say figures in English; talk about financial statements
To practise: presenting financial results

BACKGROUND: ACCOUNTING

Companies' financial statements have to give a true and fair view (not the true and fair view) of a company's profit and its assets and liabilities. This implies that there are various ways of doing accounts, and indeed there are, but companies have to adopt certain principles: in the USA, Generally Accepted Accounting Principles (GAAP), and in most of the rest of the world, International Financial Reporting Standards (IFRS), previously known as International Accounting Standards (IAS).

The *time period* principle is that accounts are always for the same length of time, usually 12 months. This prevents companies manipulating their accounts by changing the end of the financial year to disguise bad periods. The *consistency* principle states that companies have to use the same methods (e.g. of valuing depreciation and inventory) year after year. This enables investors and the tax authorities to compare one year's results with another.

The *separate entity* principle is that a company is a legal person, separate from its owners, with its own assets and liabilities. This means that stockholders have the privilege of limited liability, and if the company goes bankrupt, they are only liable for the amount they paid for their shares.

Accounts are usually prepared on the *historical cost* principle, which is that all assets are stated at the value at which they were originally brought into the company. This means companies do not need to calculate the current value of assets every year, although this can be misleading in periods of high inflation. The *going concern* principle is that a company can and will continue in business and pay its liabilities and creditors. This is why the current value of assets is irrelevant: they are not for sale.

The *matching* principle is that revenue or income is recorded in the period it is generated, along with related costs and expenditure. Examples of this principle are *depreciation* and *amortization*, which are ways of matching the cost of a long-lasting asset over the period during which it earns revenue. *Conservatism* or *prudence* means that you do not recognize any income unless you are almost certain to receive it, and you record costs as soon as they are incurred. This means that, if anything, companies should understate rather than overstate profits.

Consolidation means bringing together the accounts of all a company's subsidiaries into a single set. This allows stockholders to find out if an apparently profitable company has a non-profitable subsidiary with huge liabilities.

Lead in

These headlines all refer to genuine cases. They also suggest why accounting and auditing are important: false accounting can easily lead to companies going bankrupt, creditors and investors losing money, etc. *Scandal* (a disgraceful event causing public outrage) seems to be commonly used with both *accounting* and *auditing*.

Accounting is explained in the interview with Eric Sharp, who also suggests why both accounting and auditing are necessary: they provide information for a company's managers and investors and the tax authorities.

The answer to the second question is that there are various possible ways of doing a business's accounts.

Vocabulary 1

Most business school syllabuses include a large number of courses on accounting, so your learners may know a lot of the basic concepts. This exercise gives some basic terms that are used in the following **Listening** exercises.

VOCABULARY NOTE

Income is also known as *revenue*.

Listening 1: Types of accounting

The first question is designed to help learners understand the gist of the listening; they may need to listen more than once to find the answer.

7.1 TAPESCRIPT

Eric Sharp: In general, most of the boring work is done by purchase ledger clerks and sales ledger clerks. These are usually bookkeepers who are not qualified to a high level. The information they produce – which is basically a summary of transactions – can then be interpreted by management accountants. It can then be used by senior accountants at financial controller and director level, both for making decisions on the future of the business, and for advising other parts of the business on how to proceed.

The company's accountants also do an internal audit. The aim of this tends to be to ensure that management have sufficient internal control over what is going on. The aim of the external audit is to ensure that published financial statements give a true and fair view of the company's profit, and of its assets and liabilities.

Listening 2: Financial statements

As this exercise asks learners for specific information, ask them to read through the passage first and guess what the gapped words could be. They can then listen and check their answers.

7.2 TAPESCRIPT

Eric Sharp: There are three or four different statements that companies include in their Annual Reports, which shareholders can legally expect to see. The key documents are the profit and loss account, the balance sheet, and a funds flow statement of some kind. In the USA, and under International Financial Reporting Standards, the profit and loss account is called an income statement. This document is fairly self-explanatory: it's income less expenditure. The balance sheet is a statement showing what the company has, and what it owes at the end of the year, while the funds flow statement attempts to show whether the company is generating or consuming cash. The tax authorities require more detail than is given in these documents; taxable profit is not the same as accounting profit, so they will expect to see reconciliations between the two.

Vocabulary 2

These words are found in the financial statements of virtually all financial institutions – many of them occur in the income statement and balance sheet on the following pages.

> **ANSWERS**
> **1** 1a 2b 3b 4a 5b 6a 7c 8c 9a 10c
>
> **2** 1 consolidated
> 2 fee
> 3 commission
> 4 premiums
> 5 net
> 6 intangible
> 7 assets
> 8 intangible
> 9 assets
> 10 tax

NOTE

The financial statements are from Barclays PLC, 2005. They are available at http://www.investor.barclays. co.uk/results/2005/annualreport/annualreview2005/ downloads.htm in 'Annual Report 2005 full document' or in 'Section 3 – Results: Financial data Barclays PLC'.

Banks' financial statements obviously differ from those of most businesses, which record things like sales, and cost of sales, rather than Interest Income and Interest Expense. Interested learners will be able to find the statements of most large companies on the internet.

These statements will almost certainly contain a number of words the learners are not familiar with, but they are not essential here: this unit aims to present basic accounting vocabulary and to practise saying large figures. Some of these words (debt, equity, treasury bills, derivative instruments, etc.) are explained in later units. If learners want to know the meanings of these, they can use a dictionary or a financial website (e.g. www.investorwords.com) or use the 'define' function on Google – simply type in *define*: followed by a word, for example, *define:bond*.

Language focus: Talking about figures 1

Depending on their background (or prospective future), your learners may prefer to use either the British English or the American English way of saying figures, with or without the *and* after hundreds. Ask the learners to work in pairs for the next two tasks. Those who are calculating the figures for the first task will need some time to prepare (and a calculator).

> **ANSWERS**
> **1** 1 Total income, 2005: 17,978; seventeen billion, nine hundred (and) seventy-eight million pounds
> 2 Operating expenses, 2005: 10,527; ten billion, five hundred (and) twenty-seven million pounds
> 3 Total income: 17,978 + 15,367 = 33,345; thirty three billion, three hundred (and) forty-five million pounds
> 4 Total net profit: 3,841 + 3,301 = 7,142; seven billion, a hundred (and) forty-two million pounds
> 5 Total tax paid: 1,439 + 1,279 = 2,718; two billion, seven hundred (and) eighteen million pounds
> 6 Increase in operating expenses: 10,527 – 8,536 = 1,991; one billion, nine hundred (and) ninety-one million pounds
>
> **2** This task – calculating the number of seconds a year spent using a computer, watching television, etc. – is a light-hearted activity to practise saying large figures. Warning: some people are never the same again once they realize the number of seconds they spend at traffic lights!

Listening 3: Barclays' balance sheet

The aim of this exercise is to give learners practice listening to numbers and hearing some of the vocabulary from this unit in context. Give learners some time to look at the balance sheet and point out that the information they will hear on the CD is in a different order to the numbered gaps in the exercise. Note also that the balance sheet column is headed £m, so learners will need to convert the figures they hear into the correct format for the balance sheet, as explained in the **Language focus**.

Journalist: Large banks these days really do possess and manage vast sums of money. For example, Barclays' tangible assets – the buildings the banks are in, and so on, recorded in the accounts as property, plant and equipment – are only worth two point seven five four billion, but the group's total worth, or their shareholders' equity, is twenty-four point four three billion. Their total assets are nine hundred and twenty-four billion, three hundred and fifty-seven million pounds. Barclays' customers have deposited two hundred and thirty-eight billion, six hundred and eighty-four million pounds in their accounts, and the bank has advanced or lent its customers two hundred and sixty-eight billion, eight hundred and ninety-six million pounds. These really are huge figures.

ANSWERS

1	268,896	4	238,684
2	2,754	5	24,430
3	924,357		

Practice

The aim of this exercise is to give learners a chance to practise saying numbers and using some of the vocabulary from this unit. They can prepare a presentation in pairs. Stronger learners can invent some reasons <u>why</u> the figures have changed from the last year. If they compare the two years' figures they will need phrases like *an increase of 123 million, a decrease of 1%, increased by 2%, decreased by 3%*. This language is presented in **Units 13** and **15**.

ADDITIONAL SPEAKING ACTIVITY

An alternative practice (for learners who do not need to present to top-level directors) could involve a role play where Student A is a financial adviser or an analyst for a brokerage firm, and Student B is a (financially unsophisticated) client. Student A can advise Student B on whether Barclays is a good investment, while also explaining some of the terms found on the balance sheet.

8 Socializing

AIMS

To learn how to: greet business partners and introduce yourself; make polite conversation; talk about your career; say goodbye
To practise: socializing in English

Lead in

Learners who are still studying full-time may never have needed to use English with a visitor at work, but will probably have needed to use English out of work, where the difficulties of making 'small talk' are much the same: what to say and how to say it!

Listening 1: Greeting people and making introductions

This listening is a typical example of small talk between a visitor and host(s). Learners can listen once and answer the questions, and then listen a second time to check their answers.

⌕ 8.1 TAPESCRIPT

Michael: Excuse me, are you Mrs Steiner?

Monica: Yes. Hello.

Michael: Hi. I'm Michael. Welcome to New York.

Monica: How do you do? But please call me Monica.

Michael: Sure. Monica, do you know Siobhan?

Monica: Hello, nice to meet you.

Siobhan: Hi. How are you?

Monica: Fine, thanks. I'm sorry, I didn't catch your name.

Siobhan: Siobhan. It's Irish.

Michael: We have a car outside. Can I take your bag?

Monica: Thank you.

Siobhan: How was your flight? You must be tired.

Monica: No, I slept a little on the plane. I'm fine.

Siobhan: OK. Well, we'll take you to your hotel. Is this your first time in New York?

Monica: Oh no, I've been here a couple of times. But on vacation, not on business.

Michael: Not in November, I guess. I hope it's not too cold for you.

Monica: No, it's fine. It was almost the same in Zurich, actually.

ANSWERS

1 1 Monica has not met her colleagues before. Michael introduces himself and Siobhan.

   2 This refers to the 'non-introductory' questions which Michael and Siobhan ask Monica: *Is this your first time in New York?*
                    Can I take your bag?
                    How was your flight?

2 1 How do you do?
   2 Hello, nice to meet you.
   3 Fine, thanks.
      (The phrases used in the **Tapescript** and these responses are also shown in italics in the answer table for Question 4.)

3 *How do you do?* is a formal greeting. It is not a question requesting information; the reply is *How do you do?* On the contrary, *How are you?* is a real question, but it is often answered *I'm fine, thanks*, even if this isn't true. It is polite to return the question by asking *How are you?* or *And you?*

4

Greeting or question	Response
Hi. I'm Michael. Hello. My name is … I don't think we've met. I'm … Let me introduce myself. I'm …	*How do you do?* Pleased to meet you. Hello. Nice to meet you.
Do you know Siobhan? May I introduce you to …? Can I introduce …? Mr X, this is Mr Y. Have you met Mrs …?	*Hello, nice to meet you.* Nice to meet you too. Nice to meet you. I'm …
How are you? How's it going? (informal)	*Fine, thanks.* Fine, and you?

NOTES

The Americans are polite and informal, saying *Hi* rather than *How do you do?*

Monica does not hear (or recognize) Siobhan's name, and so asks for repetition. It is always a good idea to do this, as it becomes embarrassing to ask someone's name much later when they think you already know it.

Monica seems to speak American English. If she was speaking British English she'd have said *holiday* instead of *vacation*.

Discussion

Some cultures (particularly – or at least stereotypically – Americans, and perhaps to a lesser extent the British) seem to want to get on with business straightaway (negotiate a deal, sign a contract, get the plane home). Other cultures, notably (but not exclusively) Arab and Asian ones, want to get to know someone before doing business with them (perhaps before being prepared to trust them). This is said to be especially true in China, where people show a far greater trust in family members than outsiders.

As the aim of this activity is to promote discussion, you or your learners are encouraged to challenge these answers!

ANSWERS

There is no 'right answer' for the ranking task. However, research suggests that a typical ranking (from most time spent to least time spent) would be:

1	China	**5**	Brazil
2	Egypt	**6**	Britain
3	Japan	**7**	Germany
4	Russia	**8**	USA

1 Topics you could talk about immediately after meeting someone include:
- their journey
- where they are from
- whether they have been to your city before
- whether they like the city (if they have already been there for some time)
- where they are staying
- how long they are staying
- the weather.

2 Topics for slightly later in the business relationship include the person's family, their hobbies, and their career.

Examples of questions are given in the answers to the next exercise.

Language focus: Making small talk and keeping the conversation going

Learners can work in pairs to think of the questions for this conversation. The aim of the second task is to make learners aware of certain strategies which native speakers use in order to maintain the conversation. Learners could also think of other ways to do this and how it might be different in their own language and culture.

The general rules for doing business in a foreign language are fairly safe and not culturally specific.

> **POSSIBLE ANSWERS**
> 1   1   Is this your first visit to Dubai?
>   2   When did you arrive?
>   3   How long are you staying?
>   4   Where are you staying?
>   5   Where are you from?

> **ANSWERS**
> 2   What's it like?
>   And do you have a family?
>   And what do you do in your spare time?
>   Really? Isn't it dangerous?
>   How about tomorrow?
>
> 3   1   I'm afraid I can't make it tonight; I have another engagement.
>   2   Thank you. That sounds great.

Practice 1

See **pages 118** and **127** of the **Student's Book** for the role cards.

These are very short role plays that can be done in pairs, with maybe one or two pairs repeating them for the whole class to watch. As before, give the learners time to prepare their role and remind them to use some of the language from the **Language focus**. Each role has two meetings to practise, giving each learner the chance to be both host and visitor.

Discussion

The cultures with the strongest 'rules' of protocol or etiquette (involving bowing, the exchange of business cards, and so on) are Asian: Japan, Korea, etc.

Americans are considered to be very 'first-namey'; most Asian and European cultures are much more formal in modes of address, with even close colleagues using family names and polite verb forms after many years of working together.

In many Western cultures, people shake hands when they first meet. However, in some countries, including France, it is usual to shake hands at every meeting.

Listening 2: Talking about your career

Ask learners to read through the conversation and predict what words could go in the gaps. Then they can listen and see if they are right.

⊚ 8.2 TAPESCRIPT

Michael: How long have you worked in the finance department at Head Office?

Monica: Two years. I applied for a job there in my last year at university, when I was studying finance and economics, but I didn't even get an interview. So I went to London and worked as a trainee in a British bank for six months. After that I joined a Swiss bank, where I worked in the corporate department. Then I was transferred to their trade finance department. But I didn't get promoted so after three years I applied to this company again, and they offered me my present job. I really like what I'm doing now. I find financial planning really interesting. I'm responsible for some very big projects. What about you?

Michael: Well, I studied accounting at university and then worked for an auditing firm for two years, but I didn't like it. So I did an MBA, and then got a job here. Now, as you know I'm in production and operations. I'm in charge of setting up new production facilities here, which is why I'm working on this project with you, and I'm also involved in two projects in Canada. Which means I'm always dealing with lots of problems at the same time. But I enjoy the challenge!

> **ANSWERS**
>
> | | | | |
> |---|---|---|---|
> | 1 | applied for | 7 | accounting |
> | 2 | get an interview | 8 | auditing firm |
> | 3 | trainee | 9 | in charge of |
> | 4 | transferred | 10 | involved in |
> | 5 | promoted | 11 | dealing with |
> | 6 | responsible for | 12 | challenge |

VOCABULARY NOTES

Trainee is British English; *intern* is more common in America.

The different areas of finance mentioned in the dialogue – trade finance, asset management, fund management, trading – are not defined here; they appear again in subsequent units.

Useful phrases

Some of these phrases are from the conversation above and some are new. Learners will have the chance to practise these in the next activity.

Practice 2

This will obviously be easier if the learners have begun a career in finance, and if they know each other. If your learners are still full-time students, they can use their imagination and invent an exciting career!

This role play could also be adapted to a job interview. The learners could do the role play once, speaking in a fairly casual and informal way, like Michael and Monica in the **Listening** extract, as you would with someone you already know. Then they could do it again in a more formal way, as if they had been asked to describe their career so far in a job interview.

Listening 3: Saying goodbye

You could elicit some possible phrases for saying goodbye before learners listen to the conversation.

⊘ 8.3 TAPESCRIPT

Monica: I'm afraid I have to go now, but it's been a very useful meeting.

Michael: Of course. Yes, it's been very interesting working with you.

Monica: And I look forward to seeing you in Zurich next month. You've got my card, but let me give you my mobile number. Have you got a pen? It's 074 433 ...

Michael: 074 433 ...

Monica: ... 1991. Got that?

Michael: 1991. Thanks. If you'd like to wait in reception, the taxi will pick you up from just outside.

Monica: Ah, good. Thanks for organizing that.

Michael: No problem. See you in Zurich. Goodbye, and have a good flight!

Monica: Thanks. Bye.

ANSWERS

1. I'm afraid I have to go now ...
2. It's been very interesting working with you. It's been a very useful meeting.
3. I look forward to seeing you in Zurich next month. See you in Zurich.
4. Let me give you my mobile number.
5. If you'd like to wait in reception, the taxi will pick you up from just outside.

Practice 3

See **pages 118** and **127** of the **Student's Book** for the file cards.

The aim of this short role play is to give learners a chance to practise the language from the **Listening** exercise. Divide the class into pairs and assign each learner a role (A or B) to prepare.

ADDITIONAL WRITING ACTIVITY

If students need extra writing practice, they could write an email (as Monica or Michael) thanking the other person for the visit or their hospitality, and mentioning future contact.

9 Central banking

Lead in (including BACKGROUND)

It is useful for learners to have some background in central banking, although relatively few will ever work in this area. This exercise assumes that the learners have some knowledge of the functions of a central bank.

In most countries, one would expect the central bank to act as banker to the government and the commercial banks; decide the minimum interest rate; keep minimum deposits of commercial banks; issue banknotes; issue securities for the government; occasionally lend money to banks in difficulty; (attempt to) maintain financial stability; manage reserves of gold and foreign currencies and occasionally intervene in foreign exchange markets to (attempt to) influence the exchange rate; publish monetary and banking statistics; and supervise the banking system.

In some countries it is the government rather than the central bank that makes interest rate decisions, but there is a trend towards central bank independence. (In some countries, including Britain, the government sets the inflation target underlying interest rate changes; in other countries, such as those in the Eurozone, the central bank – in this case the European Central Bank – sets this target too.)

You would <u>not</u> expect the central bank to decide all interest rates, issue securities for companies, lend to small businesses, or to manage the assets of wealthy individuals.

In some countries – e.g. Scotland – commercial banks can also issue banknotes. In some countries the central bank is involved in clearing cheques (*checks* in US English) between commercial banks, in others

it is not. In some countries, financial supervision is undertaken by another agency; for example in Britain this role is shared between the central bank and the Financial Services Authority (see **Unit 23**).

Foreign exchange operations are covered in **Unit 13**. Most of the other functions listed above are covered in the **Listening** and **Reading** exercises below.

In answer to the second question, central bank decisions regarding interest rates have repercussions on how much people pay for their mortgage, how much they receive from savings accounts in banks, investments, etc. If the central bank is able to influence the exchange rate, this can affect the price of imports and foreign holidays.

Discussion

You could ask students to discuss this task in pairs and small groups, and then ask one student to take votes from each group to produce a class consensus on the board.

> **ANSWERS**
> 1A 2S 3S 4A 5N 6S 7N 8A 9A 10S
> 11N 12A 13A 14N 15A 16A

Vocabulary

> **ANSWERS**
> 1c 2g 3h 4a 5d 6e 7i 8b 9f

VOCABULARY NOTE
The noun *oversight* also has a more common meaning: a mistake made because of a failure to notice something.

Reading: The Bank of England

1 The text mentions the following functions from the discussion activity:
2, 4 (though it says *official interest rate* rather than *minimum*), 9, 10, 12, 13 and 16 (though it says *monitoring* rather than *supervising*).

2
1	core	6	policy
2	inflation	7	threats
3	target	8	sound
4	remunerated	9	oversight
5	sterling		

3
1 True: 'The Bank of England has two core purposes. One is ensuring monetary stability, i.e. having stable prices – low inflation ...'
2 True: 'The Government sets an inflation target ...'
3 False: 'the Bank's Monetary Policy Committee tries to meet it by raising or lowering the official interest rate ...' – the rate is not decided by the Government.
4 True: 'UK banks and building societies have to hold reserves at the Bank.'
5 False: 'These are remunerated at the Bank's official interest rate.'
6 True: 'The Bank ... can use the UK's foreign currency and gold reserves to try to influence the exchange rate if needed.'
7 False: 'The Bank has to detect and reduce any threats to financial stability' – it cannot eliminate them.
8 True: 'The Bank's role also includes oversight of payment systems ...'
9 False: 'The Bank sometimes acts as "lender of last resort" to financial institutions in difficulty' – not always.

4 identify risks
implement policies
influence exchange rates
maintain stability
reduce threats

1 identify, risks
2 influence exchange rates
3 reduce threats
4 maintain, stability
5 implements policies

Listening 1: Monetary policy

Learners can try to answer the questions in the first task before listening, based on what they have learned so far about the central banking system. They will probably need to listen to the interview more than once, and should be allowed to listen again for the third task.

🔊 9.1 TAPESCRIPT

Kate Barker: At the Bank of England, in common with most central banks round the world now, when we look at monetary policy, it involves changing interest rates.

The aim of monetary policy is to keep inflation low and stable. When you are setting interest rates, what you are trying to do is to keep demand in the economy, what people consume, how much they invest, in line with the long-term ability of an economy to supply goods and services through labour, through people employed, and through the capital employed, machinery, plant and equipment in the economy.

When interest rates rise, this will mean that individuals will tend to save more and consume less. Also for companies, investment decisions are more expensive and that means that demand will tend to be reduced. When interest rates are cut, the opposite happens – people will spend rather than save and companies have more of an incentive to invest, and that means that the level of demand rises. And it's by trying to set demand, to keep demand in line with supply in future, so that the central bank is always looking ahead.

When the central bank sets the base rate for lending to commercial banks, it affects the whole structure of interest rates in a country. For example, in the United Kingdom one of the things it affects very quickly is the rate at which the banks and other organizations lend to households for their mortgages, but of course it will also affect the rates at which companies borrow.

Of course that just means that the central bank controls the short-term interest rate. What happens to other interest rates, one-year, five-year, ten-year interest rates, can be quite different.

POSSIBLE ANSWERS

2 1 The aim of monetary policy is to keep inflation low and stable, by matching demand with supply.
   2 Changing (raising and lowering or cutting) interest rates.
   3 Consumers tend to save more and spend less, and companies tend to invest less, so demand is reduced.
   4 People tend to spend more and companies invest more, so demand rises.
   5 They change the rates at which they lend money.

ANSWERS

3	1	incentive	5	base rate
	2	plant	6	consume
	3	capital	7	demand
	4	supply	8	labour

Discussion

Keeping deposits of commercial banks implies acting as banker to the commercial banks. Although these functions are not mentioned in the exercises, central banks do also usually act as banker to the government, issue banknotes, issue securities for the government, and publish monetary and banking statistics.

ANSWERS

The **Reading** and **Listening** exercises explicitly mention:

- deciding the minimum interest rate
- keeping minimum deposits of commercial banks
- influencing the exchange rate
- lending money to banks in difficulty
- maintaining financial stability
- managing reserves of gold and foreign currencies
- supervising the banking system.

Language focus: Talking about figures 2

In American English, two-digit decimals are occasionally said as numbers (e.g. *seven point forty-seven*) especially if the number is actually a price in dollars (*Microsoft was up to fifty-eight point twenty-two*).

The difference between decimal points on the one hand, and commas after thousands on the other, is clearly important and worth stressing.

English does not use raised commas after millions, thousands, etc. (10'000'000).

Nought is British English; American English uses *zero*. Away from finance, in football scores British English uses *nil* and American English *nothing*. In tennis we say *love*.

Percent is stressed on the second syllable (per'cent), not the first.

ANSWERS

1 Right now, the euro's worth one point oh eight two nine dollars / one point zero eight two nine dollars. (With four decimal places, this number has to be expressed like this. Rounded down, it would be one dollar eight [cents]).
2 That's up nought point oh oh oh nine four from yesterday / zero point zero zero zero nine four.
3 The Bank of England's base rate is three point seven five percent.
4 Point oh oh one / point zero zero one is also called ten to the power minus three.
5 The share's trading at five dollars forty-one.

Listening 2: Saying figures

The listening contains both British English and American English speakers, so learners will hear some sentences where the speakers use *and* with hundreds (British English usage) and some without (American English usage).

⊙ 9.2 TAPESCRIPT WITH ANSWERS

1 They're buying euros at 1.4435 (one point four four three five) and selling them at 1.4935 (one point four nine three five).
2 So the spread is 0.05 (zero point oh five), or about 3.4% (three point four percent).
3 The three-month dollar rate is 2.75% (two point seven five percent).
4 Did you say 818.818 (eight hundred and eighteen point eight one eight)?

5 No, you're not listening. I said 880.808 (eight hundred eighty point eight zero eight).

6 I can't read this – is it 204,683 (two hundred and four thousand, six hundred and eighty-three) or 204.683 (two hundred and four point six eight three)?

7 He's very tall – 2.12 m (two metres twelve), and most doors are only about 2.02 m (two metres two centimetres) high.

8 Our CEO earns about 33 (thirty-three) cents a second. And there are 31,536,000 (thirty-one million, five hundred thirty-six thousand) seconds in a year.

9 Really? Let me see. That's $10,406,880 (ten million, four hundred and six thousand, eight hundred and eighty dollars).

10 That's right. And that's 246.0255319 (two hundred forty-six point zero two five five three one nine) times more than I earn!

Practice

Ask learners to work in small groups for this activity in order to give them as much speaking time as possible. They will need some time to prepare. You can also remind them to use some of the language from the **Language focus.**

POSSIBLE ANSWERS

1 In a situation like this, the central bank might let the bank go bankrupt, or hope that another bank would take it over, because although savers will lose their money in case of a bankruptcy, there might not be many further effects on the financial system. The central bank cannot be seen to underwrite irresponsible lending.

2 This would be a typical situation in which the bank might increase interest rates (if it had the power to do so), in order to slow down economic growth.

3 In these circumstances the central bank would probably try to intervene and prevent bankruptcy, as the collapse of a large universal bank would have enormous effects on the entire financial system.

4 This would be a typical situation in which the bank might lower interest rates (if it had the power to do so), in order to encourage increased spending and investment.

10 Meetings 1

AIMS

To learn how to: chair a meeting; deal with interruptions and digressions
To learn about: key vocabulary of meetings

Lead in

These questions are intended to get learners talking about their experiences of meetings. Learners at lower levels in companies are more likely to be receiving information from managers, giving progress reports to managers or to a team, or discussing day-to-day departmental matters, than making decisions in meetings with other managers of similar rank. For those learners who haven't started work yet, you could ask them about their experience of other types of meetings (such as student meetings or discussion groups).

The rest of this unit, like **Unit 12**, only considers relatively formal meetings within a company, as opposed to spontaneous, informal ones, brainstorming sessions, etc.

The cartoon seems to suggest that meetings are occasionally called for no good reason. This too could be discussed.

Discussion

It is easy enough to give rather stereotypical 'cultural tips': Northern European cultures emphasize punctuality while South Americans all show up late for meetings, Americans like to get down to business right away, Arabs prefer to make small talk and get to know you before negotiating, the Japanese prefer consensus to conflict, etc. Instead, this activity invites the learners to say what happens or doesn't happen in their own country. If the answer to the last question is 'yes', this rather negates the whole concept of cultural differences, but learners may well prefer to talk about differences among people from different parts of the world.

Vocabulary

You could do this exercise with the learners' books closed, asking questions to elicit this basic vocabulary.

> **ANSWERS**
> 1c 2f 3d 4e 5a 6b

VOCABULARY NOTE
Compromise can be a verb or a noun.

Listening 1: Chairing a meeting

With books closed, ask learners which functions the chair of a meeting usually performs. Even if learners don't have much experience of meetings, some of these, such as welcoming, inviting opinions and summarizing should be familiar. Learners can then look at the table in the **Student's Book** and, in pairs or individually, add in some phrases for each function.

VOCABULARY NOTE
The person chairing a meeting can be called the *chair*, *chairperson*, *chairman* or *chairwoman*.

> **POSSIBLE ANSWERS**
> **1** 1 Good morning everyone and welcome.
>   2 Let's get started.
>   3 The reason for our meeting today is ...
>   4 I'd like to run through the agenda.
>   5 Kim sends her apologies ...
>   6 John, would you like to say something about ...
>   7 Sorry to interrupt you, but ...
>   8 Could you just let Maria finish?
>   9 I think we're getting sidetracked here.
>   10 Thank you Robin, that was very useful.
>   11 Can I just sum up what we've said?
>   12 Can we move on to the next point?

⏺ 10.1 TAPESCRIPT

Chair: Hello, everybody. Thank you all for coming. It's nine o'clock so let's get started. This morning we're meeting to discuss all the financial aspects of moving our call centres to India. As you'll have seen, this is the main item on today's agenda.

Unfortunately, we've received apologies from Fernando Montero, our Computing Systems Director. He's stranded at an airport somewhere because of fog, so I'm afraid we'll have to continue without him.

You've all received the minutes of our last meeting. Are there any matters arising? ... OK, if no one has any comments, I'll move on to the next item and ask Alice Hewlett, Head of Customer Services, to report on her trip to India.

Alice Hewlett: Thank you. As you know, I went to Hyderabad and Bangalore last week to talk to two companies ...

> **ANSWERS**
> **2** **1** The purpose of the meeting is to discuss the financial aspects of moving the company's call centres to India.
>
> **2** b, c, e, h, i, j
>
> **3** **1** Hello, everybody. Thank you all for coming.
> **3** This morning we're meeting to discuss ...
> **6** I'll move on to the next item and ask Alice Hewlett, Head of Customer Services, to report on her trip to India ...

Listening 2: Interruptions and digressions

This is a continuation of the earlier meeting. Learners can listen once to get the gist and then a second time to pick out more details.

⏺ 10.2 TAPESCRIPT

Alice Hewlett: So, as I was saying, because the staff of both companies already speak excellent English, and have already had intensive courses about British culture, they only need to learn about our bank, and our products and services. Consequently, training costs would be very low ...

Susan: Yeah, but you're forgetting the cost of laying off all our call centre staff in Britain.

Chair: Susan, you didn't let Alice finish.

Alice Hewlett: Thank you. I'd like to add that I was easily able to find out that the starting salary for call centre staff in both cities is about 8,000 rupees a month, although the average salary is about 10,000 rupees, which is about $220. So I think that both quotes we've had are rather high, and we can easily negotiate with the companies concerned ...

Susan: Well, I'm not at all convinced it's a good thing to have our customers' phone calls answered by people who work for a subcontractor, rather than by bank staff. I think a lot of people feel this way, and this could give us a lot of bad publicity. I also think ...

Chair: I'm sorry, Susan, but that's not the question we're considering today. We're talking about the financial implications of contracting out our telephone operations. Does anyone have anything else to add on this topic? No? Well, Alice, can I just summarize the main points you've made ...

> **ANSWERS**
> **1** 6, 8, 9, 11
> **2** **8** [Susan,] you didn't let Alice finish.
> **9** I'm sorry, [Susan], but that's not the question we're considering today.
> **11** [Alice,] can I just summarize the main points you've made?
> **3** **1** False: The meeting is only about the financial implications of this possible move.
> **2** True
> **3** False: They already speak excellent English. They would only need training concerning the bank's products and services.
> **4** True
> **5** True
> **6** False. She says this move might cause adverse publicity, but this could come from journalists, political commentators, etc., rather than dissatisfied customers.

VOCABULARY NOTE
Centre is spelt the British English way here and in the **Student's Book** as this situation involves a British bank. The American English spelling is *center*.

Discussion
The interruptions in the meeting would be quite unacceptable in many Asian and Latin cultures, as anyone interrupting in this way would probably be told. There is perhaps more tolerance for such interruptions in in-company meetings in Anglophone cultures.

Language focus: Controlling meetings
The aim of this exercise is to give learners some other common phrases for controlling meetings. At the end of this section, learners should have a useful reference table (in **Listening 1**) with all of the relevant phrases.

> **ANSWERS**
> a4 b12 c6 d2 e8 f11 g8 h11 i9 j7 k10
> l9 m3 n1

NOTE
In these sentences, the chair uses first names to refer to the other speakers. This is fairly standard in America and Britain, but much less common in the rest of Europe and in Asia, where long-standing colleagues are still likely to use the equivalent of *Mr* or *Mrs* and the family name.

Practice
See **pages 118**, **127**, **132** and **135** of the **Student's Book** for the file cards.

The subject of this role play (how to improve your knowledge of finance and English) should be very familiar to all learners, whether they are working or not. The roles deliberately have conflicting ideas in order to provoke discussion and give the chair (Role A) an opportunity to practise using controlling language. Divide the learners into groups of four and assign each learner a role. Learners will need some time to prepare their role and the chair (Role A) will need to refer to the language from the unit. Give the learners a time limit for their meeting so that they can swap roles and each of them can practise being chair.

11 Financing international trade

AIMS

To learn about: letters of credit and bills of exchange; key vocabulary of letters of credit and bills of exchange

To learn how to: check and confirm information

To practise: checking and confirming information about financial products

BACKGROUND: FINANCING FOREIGN TRADE

International trade finance is a specialized, and surprisingly complicated, branch of finance. Many people working in the financial sector never have to deal with it, but if you have learners who work in the field, they can help explain things.

An excellent source of information on trade finance (at the time of writing) is the Allied Bank of Ireland Trade Finance Services' website, at http://www.aibtradefinance.com. This includes diagrams explaining letters of credit and bills of exchange, and a full glossary. This site is the inspiration behind the trade finance report in **Unit 14**.

This unit concentrates on the two most common ways of financing foreign trade: letters of credit and bills of exchange. Both of these are defined in the **Student's Book**, which also gives a complete account of the various stages involved in paying for a transaction by way of a letter of credit. More information about bills of exchange is given in the **Listening** section.

Lead in

Do this exercise with books closed, as the answer to the last question is just below in the **Vocabulary** exercise. (The answer is *letter of credit* and *bill of exchange*, and these are defined and discussed in the sections below.) If you expect the learners to know the answers to these questions, they could discuss them in pairs. If you think only a few learners will know, you could try to elicit answers from the whole class.

Vocabulary

ANSWERS
1   letter of credit
2   bill of exchange

Reading: How a letter of credit works

Ask learners to work together in pairs or small groups, using the diagram to help them.

ANSWERS
1   1   The applicant (the buyer) completes a contract with the seller.
    2   The buyer fills in a letter of credit application form and sends it to his or her bank for approval.
    3   The issuing bank (the buyer's bank) approves the application and sends the letter of credit details to the seller's bank (the advising bank).
    4   The advising bank authenticates the letter of credit and sends the beneficiary (the seller) the details. The seller examines the details of the letter of credit to make sure that he or she can meet all the conditions. If necessary, he or she contacts the buyer and asks for amendments to be made.

2   **5** When the seller (beneficiary) is satisfied with the conditions of the letter of credit, he or she ships the goods.

6 The seller presents the documents to his or her bankers (the advising bank). The advising bank examines these documents against the details on the letter of credit and the International Chamber of Commerce rules.

7 If the documents are in order, the advising bank sends them to the issuing bank for payment or acceptance. If the details are not correct, the advising bank tells the seller and waits for corrected documents or further instructions.

8 The issuing bank (the buyer's bank) examines the documents from the advising bank. If they are in order, the bank releases the documents to the buyer, pays the money promised or agrees to pay it in the future, and advises the buyer about the payment. (If the details are not correct, the issuing bank contacts the buyer for authorization to pay or accept the documents.) The buyer collects the goods.

9 The issuing bank advises the advising / confirming bank that the payment has been made.

10 The advising / confirming bank pays the seller and notifies him or her that the payment has been made.

Listening: Asking for information about bills of exchange

As there may be some unfamiliar words in this conversation (e.g. *drawer, drawee, endorsed*), ask learners to read through the questions before they listen. The meanings of the words are explained in the dialogue. Learners will probably need to listen more than once to get all the answers. After listening, ask learners if they can give any examples from their work where they have had to ask for clarification, or clarify something for colleagues or customers.

🔵 11 TAPESCRIPT

Bank advisor: Trade Finance. Can I help you?

Customer: Hello, I'm calling from Capper Trading. We've just had a large export order – our first, in fact – and we're planning to use a bill of exchange or a bank draft. Unfortunately, I'm not at all clear about some of the conditions.

Bank advisor: Well, perhaps I can clarify them for you. That's what I'm here for!

Customer: OK. Your instructions talk about the drawer, the drawee and the payee. But aren't the drawer and the payee the same thing?

Bank advisor: No. The drawer is the party that issues a bill of exchange, and the payee is the party to whom the bill is payable.

Customer: Sorry, I don't quite follow you. Surely the bill is payable to us, as we're the seller?

Bank advisor: Well, that depends whether you use a bank draft or a trade draft. A bank draft is payable to the bank. Unless you use a trade draft, issued by you.

Customer: Er, could you go over that again, please?

Bank advisor: If you use a bank draft, the buyer pays us, and then we pay the money to you, less any charges due to us. If you, the exporter, issue the bill, it's referred to as a trade draft, and it's payable to you.

Customer: Oh, I see. And if you issue the bill, it's generally payable 30, 60 or 90 days from the bill of lading date, is that right?

Bank advisor: Yes.

Customer: What exactly does that mean?

Bank advisor: The bill of lading is a document that the ship's master signs, acknowledging that the goods have been received for shipment, describing them, and giving details of where they are going. But of course you can always get the bill endorsed.

Customer: Sorry, did you say 'endorsed'?

Bank advisor: Yes, you can endorse it to the bank.

Customer: Could you explain that in more detail?

Bank advisor: Yes. We can endorse the bill before it matures. That means we guarantee to pay the bill if the buyer doesn't. Then you can sell it at a discount in the financial markets.

Customer: I don't quite see what you mean.

Bank advisor: It means you can get most of the money immediately, and you don't have to wait for the buyer to pay the bill. For example, you sell the bill at 99%, and the discount represents the interest the buyer could have received on their money until the bill's maturity date.

Customer: Oh right. OK, thank you very much.

Bank advisor: My pleasure. Goodbye.

ANSWERS

1   1   The drawer is whoever issues the bill of exchange; the drawee is the company that has to pay the amount on the bill, and the payee is the company or institution that is paid.

   2   A bank draft is issued by the bank, which receives the money (before paying it to the exporter); a trade draft is issued by the exporting company, which receives the money directly.

   3   Because they can get the bill endorsed by a bank, which guarantees to pay it if the importer does not. The exporter can then sell it on the financial markets and get the money that way.

   4   Because the buyer deducts the amount of interest it could have gained on the money until the bill matures.

2   Sorry, I don't quite follow you.
   Could you go over that again, please?
   What exactly does that mean?
   Sorry, did you say ...?
   Could you explain that in more detail?
   I don't quite see what you mean.

Language focus: Checking and confirming information

With books closed, ask learners if they know any phrases they can use when:

- they don't hear what someone has said
- they don't understand what someone has said
- they don't think someone is being clear or precise enough.

The phrases for each of these situations are listed later in the **Language focus**.

POSSIBLE ANSWERS

2   1   Could you repeat that? / I'm sorry, could you say that (last part) again?

   2   What exactly do you mean by *beneficiary*? / Could you explain *beneficiary*, please?

   3   Could you be more specific about which conditions, please?

VOCABULARY NOTE

American English uses *Pardon me?* instead of *Pardon?*

Practice

See **pages 118** and **127** of the **Student's Book** for the file cards.

The page on Incoterms is based on the Incoterms wallchart on the International Chamber of Commerce website: http://www.iccwbo.org/incoterms/wallchart/wallchart.pdf. Incoterms determine who pays for all the costs of international trade: transportation (or carriage), loading and unloading goods, insurance, customs duties, etc. The different terms, usually abbreviated to three-letter codes, are used all over the world, and so avoid uncertainties about who is responsible for paying for something – the buyer or the seller.

This role play involves a lot of reading so it would be a good idea for learners to read the document before taking on a role. Divide the learners into pairs and assign each a role (A or B). The role of the advisor at the call centre should be given to a learner who reads English quite well.

You can select one pair to perform the role play again for the whole group.

12 Meetings 2

To learn how to: conclude a meeting; ask for and give opinions; agree and disagree
To practise: holding a meeting about a call centre

Lead in

This is based on an idea from www.effectivemeetings.com. Learners can look at the quiz and discuss their answers in small groups. You could then have a whole class discussion to see if everyone agrees. Obviously, the point of the quiz is to promote some discussion, so you might need to play devil's advocate and argue for the more unusual responses!

ANSWERS
The 'correct' (most sensible) answers are 1b, 2b, 3a, 4b.

Vocabulary

The aim of this exercise is to make learners aware of some of the most common collocations associated with meetings vocabulary. Point out that the words on the left are not synonyms, although some of them are similar in meaning. When learning new vocabulary, it is useful to learn these common combinations. You will need to check learners understand the meanings of all of the correct combinations as they will need them in the next exercise.

ANSWERS
1 1 hold 2 break 3 take 4 set 5 deal with
   6 find 7 do 8 put 9 look after 10 come to

POSSIBLE ANSWERS
2 1 approve / go through, take
   2 chair
   3 circulate
   4 set, achieve / reach
   5 hold, deal with / tackle
   6 rejected
   7 put forward

VOCABULARY NOTE
While traditionally associated with meetings, *agenda* is now frequently used (especially in American English) to mean a political programme. This gives rise to other combinations, with people or parties *having an agenda*, *setting an agenda*, *carrying out an agenda*, *changing the agenda*, etc.

Language focus: Asking for and giving opinions, agreeing and disagreeing

With books closed, ask learners what phrases they know to show that they completely agree with someone, that they more or less agree with someone, and that they completely disagree with someone.

Ask learners to decide how strong their phrases are – who would they use them with (boss, colleague, friend)? You could point out that in British English it is unusual (and can be impolite) to disagree strongly with someone, especially if you don't know them very well. The British often use a more indirect style, whereas Americans tend to be more direct when disagreeing.

Learners can now look at the phrases in Question 1 for giving strong opinions, and add others for giving neutral or weak opinions.

1 Neutral

In my opinion ...
From my point of view ...
It seems to me that ...
I think / believe / feel / consider that ...
As I see it, ...
As far as I'm concerned ...

Weak

I'm inclined to think that ...
I tend to think that ...

2 Do you really think / believe that ...?
Don't you think that ...?
Are you absolutely sure / convinced / positive that ...?

These phrases can be very useful if the speaker is trying to persuade others.

3 You're absolutely right!
Exactly!
I completely agree.

4 Really? Do you think so? W
I'm afraid I don't agree. (polite) S
Nonsense! / Rubbish! (not at all polite) S
I'm not totally convinced, because ... W
I totally / completely disagree with you / with that. S
I'm afraid I can't agree with that. W
I'm against that, because ... S
I can't support that, because ... S
I don't agree. S

NOTES

To report other people's opinions, we can say *According to* (*John / Mrs X / the Financial Times*, ...). However, we do not use *According to me*, ... to report personal opinions.

I'm afraid I don't agree is strong but polite and sounds more direct, whereas *I'm afraid I can't agree with that* is weaker and sounds less direct because of the use of the modal verb (*can*).

Practice 1

See **pages 119** and **128** of the **Student's Book** for the file cards. This exercise is designed to practise phrases for asking for and giving opinions, and agreeing and disagreeing, and not to comment on learners' actual opinions. There are opinions here that various learners might agree, strongly agree or disagree with. There are others about which they may have no opinions. Divide the class into pairs and assign each learner a role (A or B). Learners will take turns to give their opinions and agree or disagree with their partner. You can stress that this is to help them practise the language and it is not a test of their real opinions.

At the end of the activity, you can ask learners to report back to the rest of the class about their partners' (real or pretend) opinions.

Listening: Concluding a meeting

With books closed, ask learners what the chair of a meeting usually needs to do at the end, and ask them if they know any phrases for these functions. There is a list of functions in Exercise 1, and a list of phrases in Exercise 2.

Play the meeting once to allow learners to get the gist. You can then play it again for them to pick up more details. Play the meeting again so that learners can check their answers.

🔘 12 TAPESCRIPT

Chair: I'm sorry, John, but I'm afraid we'll have to bring this point to a close. I think we've covered everything, and it seems that we all agree on the way ahead, so I'd like to go over the decisions we've taken.

We're going ahead with the plan to redesign and refurbish some of our branches and to relocate the others. John is going to look into the question of finding more suitable premises for the branches in List B, possibly in shopping centres, and contact property agencies. Julie will contact the company that designed our most recent branches, and also investigate their main competitors in the refurbishment business. Remember, we need a company that specializes in banks because of the security aspects, and preferably one that can arrange to do the building work out-of-hours – in the evenings and at weekends – so that normal trading can continue. Alan, you're going to see if any more market research data is available about customer expectations. Claire, you're responsible for getting more information about what facilities the back office staff in the branches in List A would like from a major modernization or upgrading.

Is that all clear? Does everyone agree with that? Good. Kirsten, you'll let us have a copy of the minutes by when – Wednesday? Good, thank you. Can we fix a date for our next meeting? I expect we need about three weeks. Can we say Monday the twenty-second, at nine?

Well, thank you, everybody, it's been a very productive morning, and I look forward to our next meeting.

ANSWERS

2　**1**　I'm sorry John, but I'm afraid we'll have to bring this point to a close.
　　2　I'd like to go over the decisions we've taken.
　　3　Is that all clear?
　　4　Can we fix a date for our next meeting? Can we say Monday 22nd, at nine?
　　5　Well, thank you everybody, it's been a very productive morning, and I look forward to our next meeting.

3　**a1　b4　c2　d2　e5　f3　g1**

4　**1**　property
　　2　Look into, evening
　　3　Look for
　　4　back office
　　5　Circulate

5　**1**　John
　　2　Julie
　　3　Alan
　　4　Claire
　　5　Kirsten

Writing

POSSIBLE ANSWER

From:　Pat Brady
To:　John.Henry@ ..., Julie.Hoyte@ ..., Alan. Walcott@ ..., Claire.Connolly@ ...
Cc:　Kirsten.Olson@ ...
Subject: Action points from yesterday's meeting

Kirsten will be circulating the minutes of yesterday's meeting shortly, but meanwhile, here's a summary of the action points and who is responsible for them.

- John will try to find shopping centre locations for the branches in List B and contact property agencies.
- Julie will look into bank redesign specialists, preferably ones that can do evening and weekend building work.
- Alan will look for market research data about what customers expect from a bank.
- Claire will find out what facilities the back office staff want.
- Kirsten will circulate the minutes by Wednesday.

Practice 2

See **pages 119**, **122**, **128**, **133** and **135** of the **Student's Book** for the file cards.

Divide the learners into groups of five, giving each member of the group a different role. As usual, give learners time to prepare their role and select a good speaker for the role of the Chief Executive, who chairs the meeting. He or she has to explain the meeting's objective, decide who can speak and when, and prevent any interruptions and digressions. He or she can also summarize other people's arguments, and decide when the meeting should come to an end. The meeting should reach a decision.

Ensure that the learners do not simply read out what is written on their role cards, or say that they disagree with an idea before it has even been suggested. The group's decision is unpredictable, and may depend on how persuasive the speakers are, or on the learners' own opinions. (However, irrespective of what your learners decide, the National Union Bank will return in **Unit 20**, negotiating with an Indian company!)

13 Foreign exchange

AIMS

To learn about: exchange rates; foreign exchange trading; key vocabulary of exchange rates

To learn how to: talk about graphs and charts

To practise: describing a graph related to your work

BACKGROUND: FOREIGN EXCHANGE

Some key dates and facts in the development of foreign exchange are given in **Reading 1**, but here are some more details:

1944   The *Bretton Woods agreement* created a system of *fixed exchange rates*. The values of many major currencies were *pegged* (or fixed) to the value of the US dollar, which was fixed at 1/35 of an ounce of gold. The American central bank, the US Federal Reserve (or the Fed), guaranteed that it could exchange an ounce of gold for $35.

1944–1971   The values of currencies were only rarely changed (*devalued* or *revalued*), with the agreement of the International Monetary Fund.

1971   The system of *gold convertibility* ended, because, due to inflation, the Federal Reserve no longer had enough gold to back the dollar.

1973   Most industrialized countries switched to a system of *floating rates*. This meant that the rates fluctuated according to *market forces*: the supply of and the demand for different currencies in international markets. However, buying or selling by speculators could cause currencies to *appreciate* or *depreciate* by several percent in a very short time. Consequently, governments and central banks occasionally attempted to influence exchange rates by *intervening* in the markets: selling huge amounts of their currency to lower its price, or using their foreign currency reserves to buy it. So there was a system of *managed floating exchange rates*.

September 1992   The Bank of England lost over £5 billion in one day attempting to protect the value of the pound sterling. Speculators were trading so much currency that it was impossible for intervention by a central bank to change a floating exchange rate.

After 1992   Governments and central banks intervened much less, so there was almost a *freely floating system*.

January 2002   Twelve states of the European Union introduced a single currency, the euro, to replace their national currencies.

Lead in

Give learners a time limit of one minute and see which learner, or pair of learners, knows the most currency names. You could also ask them to include the currencies abolished with the introduction of the euro.

The answer to the second question is given in the **Reading** text below, which also gives the recent history of many major currencies. The short answer is that, these days, the value of most currencies is determined by market forces – supply and demand.

If the learners know about their currency, and its history in terms of convertibility, fixed and floating exchange rates, etc., you could elicit and discuss the recent history of exchange rates now, before reading the text.

Reading 1: Exchange rates

ANSWERS
1944 – c   1971 – e   1973 – a   1992 – b   2002 – d

Listening: Freely floating exchange rates

As this is a challenging listening text, allow learners to listen more than once.

🔘 **13 TAPESCRIPT**

Peter Sinclair: I think a lot of people would say that there's been an important trend towards more flexibility in exchange rates. So, for example, the pound now floats freely in terms of other currencies, the central bank doesn't intervene – only very, very rarely – and that's true for an increasing number of countries.

... the market system is now doing, say in the case of sterling, what central banks and finance ministries used to do in the past, which is trying to pick and stick to an appropriate level for the currency. But there are problems with the markets: markets are not perfect. One problem is that nobody knows the future and if there is an unexpected piece of news about a country, say you discover a vast amount of oil or the government suddenly falls and is likely to be replaced by one which has a very different financial, tax, or monetary policy, then everybody will suddenly wake up and say, 'Hey this is a country whose currency we must buy lots of' or 'This is now really unsafe, we must get out.' And the swings in exchange rates can be absolutely enormous, you can see a currency go up or down by one, two, three percent maybe in a day, in response to certain news.

... a lot of the people who are operating in foreign exchange markets don't tend to think so much about the long run and what the currency really ought to be worth in order for its goods to be priced at the right level in foreign markets and so on. They're trying to guess very short-term trends, and they're trying to guess the hunches of other traders. They tend to say, 'Oh, let's see, if something is going up today it will probably go up tomorrow.' They just go in one direction and you often get huge exchange rate swings, going on for maybe even years, certainly for weeks and months, which are pushing the currency away from what it really ought to be. This is a source of worry and it's undoubtedly happening and it's due to the fact that people don't have perfect information and often tend to say, 'Well,

if he's doing this then he must know something I don't, I'd better copy him', and that can be a recipe for real trouble.

ANSWERS

1
1 Towards more flexibility, with a freely floating system and only very rare government intervention.
2 A lot of oil is discovered in a country, or the government suddenly changes.
3 There can be 'absolutely enormous' swings in exchange rates – 1, 2, or 3% in one day.
4 Because traders think about the short term, try to guess what other traders are going to do, and do the same thing (buy or sell).

2
1 the long run
2 worth
3 priced
4 foreign markets
5 short-term trends
6 hunches
7 exchange rate swings
8 worry
9 perfect information
10 recipe

3
6 *Hunches* are intuitions; ideas based on feelings.
10 If something is *a recipe for trouble* it is very likely to lead to trouble.

Discussion

You can usually find a recent exchange rate graph in financial newspapers. Explaining why exchange rates have changed will require some knowledge of recent events which your learners should be able to help you with. If your learners are already working, or are interested in this area, they could also give you some forecasts about the future.

How you could profit from exchange rate changes would depend on what currencies you currently possessed. For example, if you thought your currency would fall in value against another one, you could sell it, wait for it to fall, and buy it back again, making a profit. If you thought your currency would rise, you'd have to buy it with a foreign currency, wait for it to rise, and then sell it again for the foreign currency, so that you'd end up with more of the foreign currency. But this strategy requires possessing the other currency to start with, and buying it back later.

Reading 2: Currency trading

This text, by Frederic Madore, is widely available on the internet. The figure of 'well over US$1 trillion' a day is significantly lower than before the introduction of the euro in 2002: in the late 1990s, the estimated daily figure was $1.5 trillion. One thing this text does not mention is that a large proportion of currency trading involves forward transactions, options, currency swaps and other derivatives. These are considered in **Unit 19**.

ANSWERS

1 1 Companies and governments that buy products and services in a foreign country usually need to do so in a foreign currency. Sellers have to convert profits made in foreign currencies into their domestic currency. People need foreign exchange for travel. But most currency trading (95%) is speculative: the traders are hoping to make a profit.

2 The seven major currencies (listed in the **Reading** text) are the US dollar, the euro, the Japanese yen, the pound sterling / British pound, the Swiss franc, the Australian dollar and the Canadian dollar.

POSSIBLE ANSWERS

2 a Only 5% of all foreign exchange (Forex) trading is related to trade or business.
b The volume of foreign currency transactions is 30 times more than the volume of trading in US stocks.
c Eighty-five percent of Forex trading is in seven major currencies.
d All Forex transactions involve two counterparts (a buyer and a seller).
e On average, more than a trillion US dollars worth of currency is traded every day.
f Forex trading can be done 24 hours a day.
g Ninety-five percent of Forex transactions are speculative.

ANSWERS

3 1	turnover	**4**	speculators
2	equity	**5**	liquid
3	domestic	**6**	fluctuations

Language focus: Describing trends and graphs

A good way to demonstrate this type of language is to bring in (or ask your learners to bring in) some graphs from annual reports, a financial newspaper or the internet.

Many of the verbs in the table can also be nouns and vice versa. Also many of the adjectives can be made into adverbs by adding -ly. If learners are having difficulty thinking of other words, they could see how many of these verbs they could make into nouns, and how many of the adjectives into adverbs.

Notice that the vertical axis of the £/$ exchange rate graph goes down to $1 and not zero.

VOCABULARY NOTES

Irregular verbs: *rise – rose – risen*; *grow – grew – grown*; *fall – fell – fallen*.

The words given to describe graphs do not include verbs for huge changes (*rocket, soar, go through the roof, crash, plummet, plunge,* etc.). However, many of these appear in the **Language focus** of **Unit 15**, which looks at verbs to describe changes in stock prices.

You may want to discuss with learners how *hit bottom* and *peaked* are different to the other verbs in the table for upward and downward movement.

ANSWERS

1, 2 Answers to Question 1 are in italics – the other (possible) answers are for Question 2.

Verbs	↗	↘	→	Adjectives	Speed	Size
Verbs	*increase*	*decrease*	*level off*	Adjectives	*dramatic*	*slight*
	rise	*fall*	remain stable		*gradual*	*moderate*
	climb	drop	remain		*rapid*	considerable
	grow*	decline	constant		*sudden*	substantial
	improve*	deteriorate*	stabilize		sharp	significant
	get better*	get worse*	stay at the same level		steady	growth
					quick	rise
					slow	climb
Nouns	*growth*	*decline*		Adverbs	*sharply*	significantly
	rise	*drop*			*gradually*	substantially
	climb				dramatically	moderately
					abruptly	slightly
					suddenly	considerably
					rapidly	
					quickly	
					steadily	
					slowly	

* *grow*, *improve* and *get better* are used where upward movement is positive; *deteriorate* and *get worse* are used where downward movement is negative.

3
1 declined steadily
2 rising sharply
3 rapid fall
4 hit bottom
5 peaked
6 climbed significantly

Practice

You can either tell the learners about this in advance, and ask them to come to this lesson equipped with a graph and an explanation, or they could prepare it for the next lesson.

An alternative would be to ask the learners to imagine that they are reporting back to their boss on one of the suggested topics. The topics which are suggested should appeal to a wide range of both in-work and pre-work learners, but if your learners have other interests which can be explained with the use of graphs, they can certainly choose those.

14 Writing reports 1

AIMS

To learn how to: structure reports; separate facts and opinions; give findings, recommendations and examples; use connectors
To practise: writing a report on online trade finance

This unit returns to the (imaginary) MGS Bank, and their plans regarding the future of their retail branches, which featured in **Units 3** and **10**.

Lead in

Learners who are still studying may not have much experience of reports. Learners working in finance may already have to read and / or write them. If they are critical of some of the reports they have to read so much the better: they should then have some thoughts about what makes a good or bad report.

Some learners may be aware of the differences in style and tone among reports written for different audiences: colleagues, superiors, the board of directors, investors, the media, the general public, and so on. Reports for colleagues might be less formal than those written for superiors. Reports for an audience outside the company (investors, the media, the general public) are likely to be more polished (i.e. more work will be put into the style), to have a more positive tone (if at all possible), and to include less detail and more emphasis on what is new, good, better and potentially advantageous.

Discussion

ANSWERS
The normal order would be:
1   Title page
2   Contents list
3   Summary
4   Introduction
5   The main part of the report
6   Conclusions
7   Recommendations
8   Appendix or appendices

2, 3 and 8 are usually only necessary in quite long reports.

Reading: Facts and opinions

ANSWERS
1   Facts: 1, 2, 7 and 11
Opinions: 3, 4, 5, 6, 8, 9, 10

2   Phrases used to give opinions:
I feel …, I believe …, I have the feeling …, I think …, … it seems to me …, … in my view …, I'm inclined to think …

Useful phrases

Several of these phrases are also in the **Language focus** of **Unit 12**.

Writing 1

POSSIBLE ANSWER

Findings

Research has shown that 52% of bank customers prefer using a bank branch to using the telephone or the internet. In the richer AB social group, the figure is 45%. Our customers also want us to open longer hours, until 6 pm from Monday to Friday, and on Saturday mornings. It has also been demonstrated that well-designed and well-located branches attract more customers, who then buy more banking products. Some banks now have small coffee shops selling refreshments. Having friendly staff behind the counter is also extremely important.

Recommendations

I strongly recommend that we redesign our branches, first testing sample designs with younger customers. We ought to open branches in shopping centres, if possible incorporating coffee shops. It would be advisable to give extra training to counter staff who are not considered friendly enough with customers. I also strongly recommend opening longer hours, until 6 pm from Monday to Friday, and from 9 until 12 on Saturday mornings, though we will have to negotiate with the staff about this.

Language focus: Linking words

ANSWERS

1f 2e 3a 4d 5d 6b 7c 8c

VOCABULARY NOTE

e.g. is from the Latin *exempli gratia*, and *i.e.* is from the Latin *id est*.

Vocabulary

ANSWERS

2 1 on the contrary
   2 owing to
   3 in other words
   4 Although
   5 Furthermore
   6 Moreover, since, for instance
   7 As a result
   8 However

Writing 2

Learners will need time to prepare and write this report: it could be planned and discussed in the lesson and then given to write as homework.

POSSIBLE ANSWER

Online Trade Finance

Introduction

This report, written by ----, Head of Internet Banking, to be submitted to the Chief Executive, recommends setting up a separate Trade Finance website and introducing online trade finance facilities.

Given the success of online banking in our Retail Banking department, this report will recommend extending online banking to our trade finance services. The Trade Finance department could have its own website, giving information about trade finance, and including standardized application forms for letters of credit and bills of exchange, giving customers the possibility to start transactions and deliver instructions online.

Trade finance

Many small companies are reluctant to import or export directly, because they do not fully understand the complexities of trade finance. They would certainly appreciate a website that provided them with the information they need. This could include:

- information about import and export risks
- information about trade financing options, including letters of credit and bills of exchange
- product diagrams (flow charts) demonstrating how letters of credit and bills of exchange work
- information about Incoterms
- information about trade insurance
- answers to frequently asked questions.

Surprisingly few banks offer this service, so putting all this information online for free could create a lot of goodwill and give us a big competitive advantage. As well as offering information, the site could include:

- a list of our trade finance products and services
- details about our fees
- application forms for letters of credit, bills of exchange and other forms of payment.

At present we have several members of staff completing letters of credit and bills of exchange according to customers' instructions. If application forms were available online, and the customers filled in the details on letters of credit, reducing the amount of work necessary at the bank, this would reduce our costs and make each transaction more profitable. This increased profitability would soon cover the initial costs in setting up the website. Furthermore, offering these services would probably gain us a lot of new customers.

Conclusions

Providing this information and these online services would probably generate new business. It would also reduce the workload involved in processing customer instructions and thus significantly increase profits.

Recommendations

I strongly recommend setting up an independent MGS Trade Finance website, probably mandating a professional web design company to create it. Because of the security issues involved, this should be a company with experience in the banking sector.

15 Stocks and shares

AIMS

To learn about: stocks and shares; key vocabulary of the stock market
To learn how to: talk about market price changes
To practise: describing changes in share prices

BACKGROUND: STOCKS AND SHARES

Successful companies can issue *shares* (British English usage) or *stocks* (American English usage), which are certificates representing part ownership of a company, to raise capital to expand their operations. If these shares are offered for sale to financial institutions and the general public, this operation is called *going public*, and the business will change from a *private company* to a *public company* (called a *public limited company* or *PLC* in Britain, and a *corporation* in the US).

Offering shares to outside investors is generally called a *flotation* in Britain, and an *IPO* or *initial public offering* in the US. Companies usually get advice from an investment bank about how many shares to offer and at what price. The investment bank helps to find buyers, and will probably *underwrite* the share issue, meaning that it guarantees to buy the shares if there are not enough other buyers.

The company will commission a *due diligence report* – a detailed examination of its financial situation – from an auditing firm, and then issue a *prospectus* explaining its financial position, and giving details about the senior managers and the financial results from previous years.

Shares are also known as *equity* or *equities*. Equity financing is not the same as debt financing (borrowing money) as money raised from equities never needs to be paid back; instead the holder owns part of the business.

The most common form of equities are called *ordinary shares* in Britain and *common stock* in the US. (In Britain, *stock* means securities such as government bonds.) The people who buy equities are called *shareholders* or *stockholders*. Investors buy stocks and shares in order to receive an income in the form of annual *dividends* (a share of the company's profits), or because they hope to make a capital gain by selling the shares at a profit.

After an initial flotation, companies that require further capital can issue new shares. This is often in the form of a *rights issue*: existing shareholders are offered the first right to buy them. After shares have been sold the first time (on the *primary market*) they can be repeatedly traded at the stock exchange on which the company is listed or quoted, on what is called the *secondary market*. The major stock exchanges, such as New York and London, require listed companies to publish a lot of financial information for shareholders. The majority of companies use smaller *over-the-counter* (OTC) markets, such as NASDAQ in New York and the Alternative Investment Market (AIM) in London, which have fewer regulations.

The *nominal value* of a share (the price written on it) is rarely the same as its *market price* (the price it is being traded at on the stock exchange). This can change constantly during trading hours, because it depends on *supply and demand* – how many sellers and buyers there are. Some stock exchanges have computerized automatic trading systems that match up buyers and sellers. Other markets have *market makers*: traders in shares who quote *bid* (buying) and *offer* (selling) prices. The *spread* or difference between these prices is their profit or *mark-up*. Most customers place their buying and selling orders with a *stockbroker*, who trades with the market makers.

Shareholders' buying and selling decisions depend on the financial situation of the company, the situation of the industry in which the company operates, and the state of the economy in general, but also on the beliefs of investors – whether they think the price will rise or fall, and whether they think other investors will think this too. Although some investors keep shares for a long period, there are also *speculators* who buy and sell shares rapidly, hoping to make a profit. These include *day traders* – people who buy shares and sell them again before the settlement day: the day on which they have to pay for the shares they have purchased, usually three business days after the trade. If day traders sell at a profit before settlement day, they never have to pay for their shares. Day traders usually work with online brokers on the internet, who charge low buying or selling commissions.

Companies that make a profit are not obliged to pay a dividend to their shareholders: they can also retain their earnings by keeping the profits in the company, which causes the value of the shares to rise. Alternatively, companies can also choose to capitalize part of their retained earnings, which means turning their profits into capital by issuing new shares to their shareholders rather than paying them a dividend. There are various names for this process, including *scrip issue*, *capitalization issue* and *bonus issue*. Companies with surplus cash can also choose to buy back some of their shares on the secondary market. These are then called *own shares* in Britain and *treasury stock* in the US.

Stock markets are measured by *stock indexes* (or *indices*), such as the Dow Jones Industrial Average (DJIA) in New York, and the FTSE 100 index (often called the Footsie) in London. These indexes show changes in the average prices of a selected group of important shares.

Investors and financial journalists tend to classify shares in different categories. *Blue chips* are shares in large companies with a reputation for quality, reliability and profitability. More than two-thirds of all blue-chip shares in industrialized countries are owned by institutional investors such as insurance companies and pension funds. *Growth shares* are those that are expected to regularly rise in value. *Income shares* are those that have a history of paying consistently high dividends. *Defensive shares* provide a regular dividend and stable earnings, but their value is not expected to rise or fall very much. *Value shares* are those that investors believe are currently trading for less than they should be worth, when compared with the companies' assets. Financial journalists commonly call investors who expect prices to rise *bulls*, and investors who expect them to fall *bears*. Consequently a period when most of the shares on a market rise is a *bull market*, and one in which most of them fall in value is a *bear market*.

Discussion

If you're lucky, you'll have learners with interesting tales about speculating. If not, perhaps you can invent your own!

At the time of writing, the last major stock market crash was in 1987, which younger learners obviously won't remember. The bursting of the dot.com bubble (the end of the boom in high-tech shares) mentioned in the text occurred in 2000.

The two big 20th century crashes were in October 1929 and October 1987. The newspaper headline shown refers to the second of these. One could agree with Mark Twain that October is a very dangerous month in which to speculate in stocks, if he hadn't been making a joke about all the months of the year. Twain is famous for his novels *Huckleberry Finn* and *Tom Sawyer*, but these words of wisdom come from the main character's Calendar in his novel *Pudd'nhead Wilson*, Chapter 13. There is a further quote from Twain about speculation in **Unit 19**.

Companies issue stocks or shares, which represent part-ownership of the company, in order to raise capital to expand their operations. They usually use an investment bank for advice about how many stocks to offer and at what price, and to find buyers.

VOCABULARY NOTES

The terms *shares* and *shareholders* are used in Britain, and *stocks* and *stockholders* in the US. In Britain, *stock* also means securities such as government bonds. The terms *stock exchange*, *stock market* and *stockbroker* are used in all English-speaking countries.
The British use *company* while Americans use *corporation*.

Vocabulary 1

Reading: Why stock markets matter

This abridged article is from the BBC website:
http://news.bbc.co.uk/1/hi/business/1182349.stm.

ANSWERS

1, 2

The text answers the pre-reading question: the level of stock prices can affect consumer spending, the value of pensions, the level of employment, etc.

3 1 True: '... as stock markets fall, it is not just people who own shares who lose out ... stocks and shares have become an integral part of almost all our financial lives.'

2 False: 'Usually the first to react to this are the institutional investors ... the big City investors had already pulled out of the market.'

3 False: 'Unlike the state pension which is paid out at a rate set by the government ...'.

4 True: '... companies use ... the issue of new shares to raise capital to expand.'

5 True: '... they have to find ways of increasing the company's value to attract investors. The key tool they use is to cut jobs.'

Vocabulary 2

ANSWERS

1 1 **a** to be burnt, to suffer pain, to take a hit
     b to escape unharmed

2 1 to pull out of the market
     2 to call in a loan
     3 to attract investors
     4 to cut jobs

Language focus: Understanding market reports

If you can get hold of any financial headlines (from the *Financial Times* or a similar newspaper), it is a good way to demonstrate this type of language in context. With books closed, ask learners if they can think of any ways to describe trends which they have seen or heard in the press.

Note there are no words and phrases in Question 2 for the third column of the table – these come later in Question 4.

Learners will need to listen to the report more than once to pick out all the details.

15 TAPESCRIPT FOR QUESTION 3

Reporter: In Tokyo today, the Nikkei 225 was firmer at eight thousand, five hundred and sixty-nine point three three. Stocks around Europe also advanced this morning, following Friday's late surge on Wall Street, when the Dow Jones gained eighty points. In Paris, the CAC-40 is up twenty points, although France Telecom plunged three euros fifty to thirteen fifty-five after the company issued a profit warning, and Thomson dropped one percent to eighteen point thirty-four. The DAX in Frankfurt is also up, by thirty-six points, although Lufthansa tumbled four per cent to seven point fifteen. In London, the Footsie 100 has climbed to four thousand, two hundred and twenty point one. British Energy jumped to five pounds twelve after they published their six-monthly results. Notable losers in London, however, include Vodafone, which slumped to one pound sixteen.

On the commodity markets, copper, which seemed to be going through the roof last week, is steady at seventy-nine point seven cents a pound. Gold has slipped to three hundred and sixty-two dollars an ounce, while silver is almost unchanged at four point forty-four.

ANSWERS

2, 4 Answers to Question 2 are in italics – the other answers are for Question 4.

To go up	To go down	To stay the same
rally	*fall*	to be steady
stage a comeback	*take a beating*	to be unchanged
goes through the roof	*take a tumble*	
to be firmer	*come under pressure*	
to advance	*slide*	
to gain	to plunge	
to be up	to drop	
to climb	to tumble	
to jump	to slip	

3

1	Stocks in Japan	↗
2	Stocks in France	↗
3	France Telecom	↘
4	Thomson	↘
5	Stocks in Germany	↗
6	Lufthansa	↘
7	Stocks in Britain	↗
8	British Energy	↗
9	Vodafone	↘
10	Copper	→
11	Gold	↘
12	Silver	→

4 Verbs from the report are added to the table in Question 2 above.
Other commonly used verbs for rises include: *to be stronger, to leap (leapt – leapt), to rocket, to shoot up (shot – shot), to soar, to surge.*
Other verbs for falls include: *to be down, to be weaker, to crash, to dip, to ease, to sink (sank – sunk), to plummet, to slump, to go through the floor (went – gone).*

ADDITIONAL ACTIVITY

Ask learners which of the verbs in Question 4 could also be used as nouns.

Some of these verbs are commonly used as nouns, including: *an advance, a jump, a gain*, and *a drop* (e.g. *a jump of 3%*). Others are used as nouns in particular phrases with a verb, including *to make an advance* and *to take a tumble.*

VOCABULARY NOTE

Some of these verbs can also be used with some of the adverbs presented in **Unit 13,** e.g. *were slightly firmer / stronger, advanced slightly, gained considerably, climbed sharply, jumped dramatically, dropped substantially, fell significantly.*

Practice 1

See **pages 119** and **128** of the Student's Book for the file cards.

The learners can prepare these roles in pairs, but they should be careful not to show their graph to their partner. Learners will need a clean sheet of paper and a pencil (rather than a pen!) to draw their partner's graph. If you have a more advanced group, or one which needs to use the phone, this practice can also be done as a telephone call, although it is more challenging. Learners should be encouraged to ask questions about why the changes occurred, and to think of possible reasons (or invent them) for their own set of figures.

Practice 2

Obviously, the longer the imaginary portfolio is in existence, the more chance it has of gaining or losing value. This exercise will not work as well on a five-day intensive course!

You could provide lists of the leading blue-chip companies on leading stock exchanges, easily available in the financial press, and perhaps details of companies that have only recently gone public (offered their stocks for sale).

If the learners buy stocks in other currencies, remember to record the exchange rate used.

With more motivated learners, it may be possible to change the rules, and allow them to buy and sell during the period that the portfolio is in existence (charging, say, 2% commission for each transaction). They can be asked to explain the reasons for the positions they have taken.

16 Writing reports 2

AIMS

To learn how to: use the right style and tone; use the right presentation and layout
To practise: writing a complete report

Lead in

In-company teachers may already know the answers to these questions. If your learners come to a school, the answers to these questions might explain why some come with smiles on their faces and others not! If your learners are full-time students who are not yet in professional life, the questions could be rephrased to ask what amenities they would like or expect in their first job.

Reading: Head Office relocation

This unit is based on real data from a large international bank which moved 8,500 staff from 21 different offices in the City of London to a new, 44-storey tower a few miles away in Canary Wharf in 2002. Here, the situation has been transposed to the fictional Metropolis Bank in New York.

Learners should read through the questionnaire and then the class can discuss the following questions.

VOCABULARY NOTE

Learners may not know the word *inoculations* – British English uses *vaccinations*.

Discussion

As always, learners can discuss these questions in pairs or groups, and then you can see if there is any consensus. Even if there are widely varying opinions about the facilities in a company or business school, this is still useful language practice.

Listening 1: Catering choices

Learners will need to listen to the dialogue more than once to pick up all the details. The word *catering* (providing food; used in the title, but not in the dialogue) may need explanation.

16.1 TAPESCRIPT

Project Manager: So, any surprises?

HR manager: No, not really. Well, yes, actually – the response rate. It was extremely high. We sent the questionnaire to about 50% of the staff, and got nearly 3,200 responses – that's around 80%.

Project Manager: That's very good. So what do they want?

HR manager: Food! And lots of it! There's a clear demand for both a staff restaurant, serving hot and cold lunches, and for coffee and sandwich shops. Most respondents already working in departments with restaurants say they only eat out once a week, on average. But they also say they wouldn't choose the same lunch option every day. They clearly expect a building with 8,000 people working in it to provide them with several choices.

Project Manager: Well that's OK, isn't it? That's more or less what we're already planning.

HR manager: Yes, but there's also a significant demand for breakfast as well – both cooked breakfast and coffee and pastries. Though on the other hand around 30% said they were likely to bring in their own lunch most days, and would like fridges and microwaves near their offices.

Project Manager: That's fine – it still leaves over 5,000 people to feed. And breakfast is no problem once you have the staff and the facilities. At the moment we're thinking of an 850-seat restaurant, serving around 2,500 meals daily, about three-quarters at lunchtime. In fact it'll be one of the largest restaurants of its kind in the country. In the world even.

ANSWERS

1 1 Because 80% is an extremely high response rate for a questionnaire of this kind.
   2 Four, on average
   3 Around 30%
   4 850 seats, serving around 2,500 meals a day

2 The basic information coming from the questionnaires is that:
   • The staff want a restaurant, serving hot and cold breakfasts and lunches, as well as coffee and sandwich shops.
   • Most staff only go out to eat at lunchtime once a week.
   • About 30% bring in their own lunch.

Listening 2: Health and leisure needs

Allow learners to listen to the dialogue twice to pick out all the information.

🎧16.2 TAPESCRIPT

Project manager: OK, what was next?

HR manager: Well, after they've eaten they seem to want to sweat it off! Over 90% are in favour of a gym, especially the female respondents. They want rooms for a range of exercise classes (aerobics and yoga and things), as well as full gym equipment like weights and running machines. Less than 20% asked for squash or badminton courts, so I'm not sure we need to plan those, but – wait for it – about 50 people said they would like a swimming pool!

Project Manager: A swimming pool? Where do they think we're going to put that?

HR manager: Er … on the roof!

Project Manager: Oh dear, I think we're going to have to disappoint 50 people! Now, tell me about medical and healthcare.

HR manager: Well, I was a bit surprised, but hardly anyone expects a diagnostic doctor service or dental treatment. Most people said they prefer to have only one doctor, and to get treatment near where they live. There were also concerns over patient confidentiality.

Project Manager: Yes, that doesn't surprise me. Most people don't want their employer to have access to their medical records. I guess we'll simply abandon that idea.

HR manager: Yet over 65% were in favour of a health clinic for things like travel advice and inoculations. And 8% want cycle parking and changing facilities. This is higher than we expected.

Project Manager: These people who cycle in Manhattan – they amaze me. But we'll clearly have to do something about that. Eight per cent of 8,000 is a lot. Anything else?

HR manager: Well, 200 people want their own space in an underground parking lot, even though we specifically said this isn't an option.

Project Manager: I can understand that – I'd like one too! But like you say, we can't even think about that.

HR manager: And about 100 people – I know that's not a lot – want a convenience store where they could get things like newspapers and magazines, candy, cans of soda and 'emergency' purchases like tissues and headache tablets. I guess 8,000 customers is enough for a store like that; they have them in hotels with much fewer people.

Project Manager: True, but we're not building a hotel. Our people will be working and not shopping most of the day. Anything else?

HR manager: Yes, the 'Do you have any other concerns?' question showed that there are a number of things the staff are worried about. Understandably, a lot of respondents voiced fears about a terrorist attack, and want a lot of information about evacuation arrangements and fire precautions. I think we'll have to send everybody a special booklet about this, explaining what the architects are doing.

Project Manager: Yes, that's a good idea.

HR manager: And a lot of people seem to be worried about the time it will take to move around within the building. Most of them have never worked in a forty-storey high-rise, and certainly not in one with so many people working in it. This building is going to take some getting used to.

ANSWERS

1
1 A swimming pool and reserved car parking.
2 There is a strong demand for a fully-equipped gym and rooms for a range of exercise classes, and much less demand for squash and badminton courts.
3 They prefer to go to only one doctor, situated near where they live, and they are worried about patient confidentiality – the risk of their employer having access to their medical records.
4 To have a convenience store selling newspapers, magazines, candy, soda, etc.
5 It is about fire precautions and evacuation arrangements in case of an emergency or a terrorist attack, because this seems to worry a lot of people.
6 The time it will take to move around a large, 40-storey building holding 8,000 people.

2 The staff want:
• a fully-equipped gym and rooms for a range of exercise classes
• a health clinic for things like travel advice and inoculations
• cycle parking and changing facilities
• a convenience store
• information about evacuation arrangements and fire precautions.

The staff do not want a diagnostic doctor service or dental treatment.

VOCABULARY NOTE

Leisure is pronounced /'leʒə/ in British English and /'liːʒər/ in American English.

Writing 1

Learners can work in pairs or small groups to decide on the information they need to include in the report. They should refer back to **Unit 14** for an example of an introduction and terms of reference.

The outline could be written in note-form as a series of bullet points. It would contain the information shown below (arranged in a paragraph here), which could serve as the summary.

POSSIBLE ANSWERS
Introduction
This report, written by ----, Relocation Project Manager, to be submitted to the Chief Executive, summarizes the responses to our Relocation Questionnaire. The response rate was surprisingly high, at around 80%, meaning that nearly 3,200 responses were received.

The questionnaire asked questions about a number of specific facilities, relating to eating, exercise, healthcare and travel to work. It also invited staff to raise any other concerns, make other requests and express other preferences.

Summary
This report summarizes 3,200 responses from our staff to the Relocation Questionnaire. There is heavy demand for a restaurant, serving both breakfast and lunch, as well as coffee and sandwich shops. This is very much in line in what has already been planned. There is also demand for facilities for staff members who bring in their own food. There is high demand for a gym and exercise rooms, and less demand for squash and badminton courts. The staff would also like a health clinic, cycle parking, and a convenience store. The report recommends providing all these things. There is very little demand for a diagnostic doctor service or dental treatment, so we need to reconsider these plans. The staff want information about evacuation arrangements and fire precautions. It is recommended that we produce an information booklet about this.

Language focus: Style and tone

The first text is clearly a press release or a public relations document, destined for the general public or perhaps the bank's customers. It is full of subjective adjectives (*award-winning, breathtaking, cutting-edge, state-of-the-art, fully-equipped, multi-purpose, high-tech* and *top-notch*), most of which should generally be avoided in any other sort of writing. (For example, *state-of-the-art* simply means latest; *cutting-edge* means leading, pioneering or progressive.)

It contains information that is of little intrinsic interest, but sounds impressive, such as the quantity of steel, concrete and glass.

A document intended for use inside the company, or for investors, would be more factual, with fewer adjectives.

The second text is clearly an email or memo to a colleague, written in a very informal style. It contains colloquial expressions such as 'the picnic people' for staff who bring their own food to work, and 'cross that one out'.

It uses ellipses: 'worries about confidentiality' for 'There were worries about confidentiality', and dashes, exclamation marks and expressions like 'Well' and 'I mean'.

None of this would be done in a formal report.

Writing 2

1 All the subjective adjectives are listed in the **Language focus** above.

Metropolis Bank has announced that its headquarters will be moving to a new 40-storey tower in the Financial District next summer. The new building, designed by the Godwin-Malone partnership, will contain over 1 million square feet of office space, to house 8,000 employees. Facilities will include an enormous 850-seat staff restaurant and a multi-purpose gymnasium offering staff personalized training programs.

2 Here are the results from the questionnaire:
   - Lots of people want a restaurant for breakfast and lunch.
   - Lots of people want coffee and sandwich shops.
   - People who bring their own lunches want fridges and microwaves.
   - Lots of people, especially the women, want gym and exercise classes.
   - Not many want squash or basketball courts.
   - Some people want a swimming pool.
   - Very few want doctors or dentists on site.
   - A lot of cyclists want cycle parking and somewhere to change.
   - Some people want a convenience store.

As most of this is already planned, we should be able to get started straight away.

Writing 3

Learners can use their notes from the **Listening** exercises and from the second task in **Writing 2** above as a basis for the main part of the report. A model Summary and Introduction have been given in **Writing 1** above. Possible versions of the Findings, Conclusions and Recommendations are shown below.

POSSIBLE ANSWERS

Findings

Most respondents want to eat lunch in the new building. At present, they only eat out once a week on average. But they would not choose the same lunch option every day, and so expect a choice of restaurants, coffee shops and sandwich shops. Around 30% said they were likely to bring in their own lunch most days.

Over 90% are in favour of a gym, especially the female respondents. They want rooms for a range of exercise classes (aerobics, yoga), as well as gym equipment such as weights and running machines. Fewer than 20% of respondents expressed an interest in squash or basketball courts.

Hardly anyone expects a diagnostic doctor service or dental treatment. They prefer to have only one doctor, and to get treatment near where they live, and they are concerned about patient confidentiality. Yet over 65% were in favour of a health clinic for things like travel advice and inoculations.

Cycle parking and changing facilities were requested by 8% of respondents. A small number of respondents want a convenience store (selling newspapers, magazines, candy, soda, tissues, headache tablets, and so on).

A lot of our staff are worried about a terrorist attack on the new building, and want detailed information about evacuation arrangements and fire precautions. A number of people also appear to be worried about the time it will take to move around within the building.

Conclusions

The staff has fairly explicit preferences regarding food and leisure activities, which are more or less in line with what we expected and have already planned. The demand for cycle parking and changing facilities is higher than we imagined. There is a fairly high level of anxiety about the possibility of a terrorist attack on the new building, and a strong demand for information about evacuation procedures and fire precautions.

Recommendations

- Go ahead with the planned 850-seat restaurant, serving both breakfast and lunch.
- Add several smaller coffee and sandwich shops.
- Ensure that there are facilities for people to store, heat and consume their own food.
- Install a fully-equipped gym and rooms for a range of exercise classes.
- Consider setting up a health clinic for travel advice, inoculations, etc., but abandon plans to have full-time doctors and a dentist.
- Expand the planned cycle parking area; ensure that adequate changing facilities are available (probably in the gym).
- Analyse the viability of a convenience store.
- Write and send everybody a booklet about planned evacuation arrangements and fire precautions.

NOTE

If you have an example of a very badly laid-out and presented document you could perhaps show it to the class, if this doesn't breach anybody's confidentiality.

17 Mergers and acquisitions

To learn about: mergers and acquisitions; key vocabulary of mergers, takeovers and buyouts
To learn how to: talk about cause and effect
To practise: talking about the effects of takeovers

BACKGROUND: MERGERS AND ACQUISITIONS

Various sections of this unit in the **Student's Book** – the **Reading**, the **Listening** and the example of P&G and Gillette in the **Language focus** – contain a fairly complete account of what mergers and acquisitions are, why they exist, and how they are carried out.

Lead in

The headlines will provide a good way in to the topic and if you or your learners can find some up-to-date examples from the financial press, that would provide a further discussion topic, as well as a good example for the last question. Most business learners can be expected to know the concepts involved here even if they do not know the English words *merger, takeover, bid, raid* and *hostile*. All these questions (except the last one) are answered in the **Reading** text.

VOCABULARY NOTES

The noun *takeover* is one word, the verb *take over* is two.
Irregular verb: *bid – bid – bid*.
Most people (including journalists) talk about *takeovers* rather than *acquisitions*, but investment banks have Mergers and Acquisitions departments.

Reading: Mergers, takeovers and buyouts

The aim of this activity is to help learners pick out the main point of each paragraph. You could give them a time limit to do this activity.

> **ANSWERS**
> 1d 2e 3b 4a 5c

Vocabulary

After doing this exercise, you could ask the learners to explain the newspaper headlines. If the learners were not able to answer the questions in the opening **Discussion** activity before reading the text, you could return to this exercise after completing the **Reading** and **Vocabulary** activities, doing it as a comprehension exercise.

> **ANSWERS**
> 1 diversifying
> 2 market share
> 3 economies of scale
> 4 fees
> 5 customer base
> 6 optimum
> 7 synergy
> 8 raiders
> 9 conglomerates
> 10 asset-stripping

Listening: The role of banks

Peter Sinclair, who is also interviewed in **Units 1**, **3**, **13** and **19**, is the former director of the Centre for Central Banking Studies at the Bank of England. The pre-listening **Vocabulary** activity will introduce learners to new words which they will hear in the interview. The phrases *buying spree* and *drum up business* are more informal.

Learners will need to listen to the interview more than once to check their answers. When they have completed the exercise, they could look at the **Tapescript** and pick out the words from the first exercise to see how they are used in context.

Peter Sinclair: Well, the role of the investment banks; yes, they're certainly big, important players in mergers and acquisitions, and yes, they may sometimes try and drum up business, but I think that no well-run firm will want to engage in this kind of activity unless they see merit in doing so. So it isn't all driven by the banks.

What we do note – and that is really interesting – is that when a company goes for a takeover, tries to take over another, the thing that's most important is its share price, the share price of the company doing the takeover. So if the share prices do well – which they did in the 80s and 90s, most of the time – companies feel richer, their shares are more valuable, so they tend to go out on a buying spree and they will get advice from big investment banks and merchant banks about when to buy and what to buy. And the potential victim of a takeover bid will obviously want to get advice from another national institution about how to defend itself, assuming that's what it wants to do.

So we've seen a lot of acquisitions and mergers, some friendly mergers and some contested takeovers, a lot of them happening in a strong stock market. In the early twenty-first century, so far, we have been seeing share prices slide a bit and so mergers and acquisitions are becoming less frequent and of course less valuable. The value of companies has fallen so the value of the activity for the merchant banks, investment banks, has been slipping too. It is very much a cyclical phenomenon – boom for shares means more takeovers, slump for shares means less.

ANSWERS

1 1b 2d 3e 4a 5c
2 1 True: '... they may sometimes try and drum up business.'
   2 False: '... no well-run firm will want to engage in this kind of activity unless they see merit in doing so.'
   3 True: '... if the share prices do well ... their shares are more valuable, so they tend to go out on a buying spree.'
   4 False: '... which they did in the 80s and 90s, most of the time.'
   5 False: '... they will get advice from big investment banks and merchant banks about when to buy and what to buy.'
   6 True: '... the potential victim of a takeover bid will obviously want to get advice from another national institution about how to defend itself.'
   7 False: '... so the value of the activity [advising on takeovers] for the merchant banks, investment banks has been slipping' – but not necessarily the value of the banks themselves.

Language focus: Cause and effect

Before doing the exercise, you could find out what learners know about the two companies, Gillette and Proctor & Gamble. Financial journalists have described the event as both a *merger* and an *acquisition*, although the P&G website uses the term 'merger'.

POSSIBLE ANSWERS

The takeover announcement *led* to a 13% rise in Gillette's stock price.
P&G predicted that the merger would *bring about* cost savings of between $14bn and $16bn.
The merger *resulted in* a 27% increase in sales but also 6,000 job losses.
The FTC gave its approval *so* the merger could go ahead.
Both companies had to sell off some product lines *because of* the merger.

VOCABULARY NOTES

Irregular verbs:
bring – brought – brought; lead – led – led; mean – meant – meant; arise – arose – arisen

Practice 1

Learners can work in pairs for this exercise. They should use the work-related graph which they produced in **Unit 13, Practice 1**. This is a good opportunity to review the trends language from both **Unit 13** and **Unit 15**.

Practice 2

See **pages 119**, **122**, **129**, **133** and **135** of the **Student's Book** for the file cards.

If you have more than five learners, they can prepare the roles in groups. Select good speakers for the role of the Chief Executive, who chairs the meeting, and ensure that the learners do not simply read out their role.

The actual meeting can be quite informal. There is only one item on the agenda, and the participants all know each other (although it is good practice in the role play for them to introduce themselves).

The group's decision could go in various directions, depending on how persuasive the speakers are.

VOCABULARY NOTES

There are two specific phrases in the role cards which should be explained. A *white knight* (Role B, Head of Corporate Banking) is a person or organization that rescues one company from being bought by another when the suitor is undesirable or the price too low. A *poison pill* (Role D, Human Resources Director) is a form of defence that a company can use when another company is trying to take it over: to make itself less attractive it can sell off some assets, increase its share capital, etc.

Writing

Learners might also want to look back at the **Language focus** in **Unit 14** to help them structure their report.

POSSIBLE ANSWER

One possible outcome of the meeting could lead to the following report to the Board.

> We believe that we should recommend the proposed takeover of MGS Bank by the National Union Bank to our shareholders, on condition that the National Union Bank agrees to our continuing to use our name as part of their financial services group. In the current climate of consolidation in the financial industry, the small size of our bank probably makes a takeover inevitable. Furthermore, we know that the majority of our shares are owned by institutional investors who support the bid. The takeover will give our bank access to more capital and provide considerable protection against bad debts. Continuing to trade under our old name will allow us to retain our regional character and our good local reputation.
>
> The meeting discussed but rejected other alternatives, including looking for a white knight, and conducting a poison pill defence by issuing new shares to our existing shareholders at a large discount.

18 Negotiating 1

AIMS

To learn how to: negotiate; make, accept and reject proposals, counter-proposals and conditional offers

To practise: making conditional offers and negotiating the conditions of a commercial loan

Lead in

These questions are designed to promote discussion.

- If learners don't think they have to negotiate outside of work, ask them to think about buying a car, getting a loan from the bank, or even deciding on a holiday destination with their friends or partner – all of these involve negotiation.

- Some learners may not have to participate in formal negotiations, but will probably be involved in more informal discussions – persuading team members about a proposal, asking for extra time off work and asking a colleague to do you a favour are some examples.

- There are no hard and fast rules as to what makes a good negotiator, as there are countless different types of negotiation: defusing a nuclear weapons crisis, securing the release of a hostage, preventing a threatened strike, securing a one-off deal to supply or receive goods or services, and putting the finishing touches to a merger or joint venture all require different abilities. Yet it is generally argued that good negotiators are well-prepared, with clear objectives, strategies and agendas; are good speakers and even better listeners; are good at clarifying anything they don't understand; are courteous and polite; are creative and flexible when bargaining; and try to avoid confrontation and to reach a position of mutual advantage.

- It is generally felt that many of these skills can be learnt, although clearly some personality types are better than others at negotiating.

Vocabulary

ANSWERS
1c 2j 3f 4e 5h 6g 7a 8i 9b 10d

Reading: Learn to Love Negotiating

This text is shortened from http://www.creativepro.com/story/feature/17093.html.

Let learners read the text (you may want to give them a time limit) to see if they can get the gist. If they have done the previous **Vocabulary** exercise, there shouldn't be many unknown words, but you can stress that they don't need to understand every word.

ANSWERS
1 The tip that is probably the most difficult to put into practice is 'Always have a good idea in advance of how you'll respond if things do not work out as you plan.' It's hard to know how you will respond when you don't know what you will be responding to.
2 1c 2d 3a 4b 5e
3 Two – c and d

Language focus: Making proposals, counter-proposals and conditional offers

Listening 1: Conditional offers

Learners can listen once without writing anything and then a second time to pick out the details.

●18.1 TAPESCRIPT

Administrative Director: OK, I'm going to be direct about this. We need your offices to use as conference rooms for meetings with customers. I'm sorry to say this, but they're much too nice for an IT department! So we're asking you to relocate to some offices we've rented across the street. Of course this is only temporary, as we're all moving to the new building in a year's time.

IT Manager: And why can't you use the offices across the street as meeting rooms?

Administrative Director: Because they're a bit small. And dark. Two of them don't actually have any windows.

IT person: You must be joking. We couldn't agree to that. Why would we go there?

IT Manager: No, wait a second. We would consider a temporary move on condition that we get much larger offices in the new building.

Administrative Director: I'm afraid 'much larger' is out of the question. But we'd be happy to discuss the size of your offices in the new building as long as we can have your current offices before the end of the month.

IT Manager: I'm afraid we can't accept that. Discussing the size will not be enough. I say 'much larger' because as you know we are understaffed. We would agree to move temporarily provided that we got the go-ahead to hire the software designer and the systems analyst we need. Who would obviously require offices.

Administrative Director: Well, we could offer you two extra offices, so long as no other department objects, but as you know I can't make staffing decisions.

IT Manager: I'm sorry, but we wouldn't consider moving now unless you can guarantee us both the staff and the space we need.

Administrative Director: Well, I'd be willing to take your request to the next Board meeting if you agreed to move out on the 26th. What would you say to that?

IT Manager: I'm afraid that still doesn't meet our requirements.

Practice 1

See **pages 120** and **129** of the **Student's Book** for the file cards.

Divide the learners into pairs, assigning each a role (A or B). Give them some time to read through their demands and to decide what their limits are. Learners will need to be flexible about their demands, so they should be able to reach a compromise. The idea is to practise bargaining using conditional proposals, as in the **Listening** exercise.

Listening 2: Should we grant this loan?

Learners can listen to the conversation once for gist, and then a second time to pick out the details.

◉ 18.2 **TAPESCRIPT**

Sally: So, Chris, the situation is this. Capper Trading has the exclusive rights to manufacture Moggles toys, to go with a new children's cartoon series on the television. I don't know if you've heard of it ...

Chris: No.

Sally: Well it goes out every day, early in the evening, and the kids seem to love it, and the toys based on the series – they're little plastic figures – are selling really well. But Capper can only produce 20,000 a week. They don't want to take on extra staff and run two shifts in the factory, because they don't know how long these toys will go on selling. So they want to sub-contract to a company in China, and they want to start immediately. They have a company lined up, but they're going to have to pay them 60 days after the first shipment, and they don't have a big enough cash flow.

Chris: OK, so how much cash do they currently have?

Sally: Well, none. But that's because they're too successful! They've spent all their money on raw materials, and they're making these toys, and they're selling as fast as they can supply them, but the wholesalers haven't paid them yet, and they need to import more.

Chris: Have they got firm orders for the toys they want to import from China?

Sally: Yes. For 100,000 toys. But they're sure they'll soon get more orders, when the first ones sell out. They want to import 500,000.

Chris: Yeah – and what happens if suddenly the series isn't popular any more or all the kids have got the toys, and your company – what are they called?

Sally: Capper Trading.

Chris: And Capper Trading has to pay for up to half a million toys they can't sell, that they've bought with our money?

Sally: They don't think that's going to happen.

Chris: Of course they don't. But it could, couldn't it? Look, bring them in, let's have a meeting tomorrow afternoon.

> **ANSWERS**
> **Company:** Capper Trading
> **Company manufactures:** Toys based on a new children's TV cartoon series but can only produce 20,000 a week
> **Company wants to sub-contract to:** A Chinese manufacturer
> **Has orders for:** 100,000
> **Wants to import:** 500,000
> **Meeting arranged for:** Tomorrow afternoon

Discussion

Learners will need to think about the risks involved and the potential benefits of granting the loan. You could also refer them back to **Unit 5** which discusses lending criteria.

Practice 2

See **pages 120** and **130** of the **Student's Book** for the file cards.

The aim of this activity is for learners to practise negotiating in a financial context.

The bank (Role A) are considering granting the loan, but they are concerned that if the toys stop selling, the company could have paid for 100,000 unwanted imported toys, on top of the 20,000 a week it is manufacturing itself. They therefore need to charge a high interest rate, and prefer an arrangement that gives them greater security (a loan secured by specific assets). The potential benefit for the bank is a successful and profitable new business customer.

Capper Trading (Role B) are convinced they have a very

good commercial opportunity: the exclusive rights for toys linked to a very successful children's cartoon series. They need short-term credit (30–60 days) to pay the Chinese sub-contracted manufacturers while Capper wait for payment from their wholesalers. They have approached MGS Bank because their advertising states that they want to help local businesses. If Capper's new product is as successful as they think it is going to be, working with Capper will be good for the bank's reputation.

Learners can prepare this role play in two groups: As and Bs. This will give them a chance to think about their arguments and questions for the other side. They can then do the activity in pairs (A and B) or in small groups with two or three learners on each team. If there is time, you can select some learners to act out their role play in front of the class. The result of the meeting depends whether one side can convince the other to modify its position.

Writing

POSSIBLE ANSWER

This email could be sent after a successful negotiation. The content will depend on what was agreed.

From: Sally Raven
To: Simon King
Cc: Kirsten.Olson@ ...
Subject: Summary of our meeting

Dear Simon

It was very good to meet you yesterday. Following our discussion, here is a summary of the main points.

-
-
-
-

19 Derivatives

AIMS

To learn about: futures, options and swaps; key vocabulary of derivatives

To learn how to: clarify, summarize and paraphrase

To practise: talking about the advantages and disadvantages of derivatives; clarifying and summarizing key points from a talk

BACKGROUND: DERIVATIVES

The text in the **Student's Book** contains the basic information about derivatives. Here are some additional details and terms.

Commodities for which there exist *futures markets* include wheat, maize, soybeans, pork, beef, sugar, tea, coffee, cocoa, orange juice, oil, precious metals (gold, silver, platinum) and non-precious metals such as copper, aluminium (*aluminum* in American English), etc.

Trading in *financial futures* began in Chicago in 1972 with futures in currencies. *Interest rate futures* were first traded in 1975, and *stock market index futures* in 1982.

The buyer of an *option* is said to have a *long position*, and the seller a *short position*. The price at which the asset underlying an option can be bought or sold is called its *strike price* or *exercise price*. A *call option* with a strike price below the current market price of the underlying stock price is said to be *in-the-money*. A *put option* is *in-the-money* if the stock price is below the strike price. Conversely, a call option is *out-of-the-money* if the exercise price is above the market price of the underlying stock, as is a put option if the exercise price is below the market price of the underlying stock. In these cases the options have no intrinsic value.

So-called *American-style options* can be exercised at any time between the purchase date and the expiration date. *European-style options* can only be exercised on their expiration date.

Derivatives are risky (or positively dangerous) investments for various reasons. Although two parties can choose to hedge against a particular risk, only one of them can actually make money from the contract: prices, interest rates and exchange rates cannot simultaneously rise and fall. And speculatively writing or selling options is extremely risky, as there can be huge

changes in the price of an asset or a currency during the term of the contract. Furthermore, options give huge *leverage*; for a small amount of capital – the price of a few options – an investor can become exposed to enormous price changes in the underlying derivative asset.

Lead in

The main types of derivatives are futures, options and swaps. These are all defined in the **Reading** text, as are the two main uses of derivatives, which are hedging and speculating. Learners working in organizations that use or trade derivatives may already know a lot about them; those working in different types of jobs may not, though derivatives feature quite regularly in the press.

Reading 1: Derivatives

ANSWERS

1	1	put option	6	interest rate swap
	2	commodities	7	exercise
	3	futures	8	speculator
	4	call option	9	premium
	5	hedge		

2 determine prices
eliminate risks
exercise options
guarantee prices
reduce risks
reduce uncertainty
swap interest payments

1 swap, interest payments
2 eliminate, risks
3 reduce risks / uncertainty
4 options, exercise
5 determine / guarantee prices

Listening: Derivatives

As some of these questions (2, 5, 7) require learners to explain some quite complex language and concepts, you should allow them to work together to answer these.

For Question 7, some learners may disagree with the idea that financial institutions should necessarily take risks. However, most banks are prepared to take some (calculated) risks, as discussed in **Unit 5**.

⊙ 19 TAPESCRIPT

Peter Sinclair: Derivatives are a very mysterious phenomenon. They are not entirely new but there has been an enormous growth in them recently, and what they are is funny kinds of financial trick which change the structure of risks and returns. Often they promise higher return on average but at the cost of big increase in risk, that's their usual property.

OK, so who buys them and why are they undertaken? Sometimes people undertake financial derivative transactions actually to make themselves safer, to hedge. They've got a bill, let's say, coming up, which has to be paid in US dollars. Well, the sensible thing to do is try and hold some US dollar assets ahead so that if, when the day comes when you have to pay this US dollar bill, the dollar hasn't in the meantime gone up very sharply, which could spell real trouble for you. So hedging is actually an important source of demand for derivatives; and companies can, in appropriate circumstances, make their financial position much stronger and much safer by undertaking these activities. But these derivatives are complicated, they certainly may not be fully understood even by the banks which are rather keen on doing trades in them.

Steve Harrison: You have to adopt a balanced view of derivatives, because they have had a very bad press. There have been some very well-cited examples of misuse of derivatives, and these have caused problems in the market – potentially they could have caused a lot of dislocation in various markets. But I think we need to recognize that derivatives have been around for a very long time, in various formats, and that used properly they can be a very helpful financial management tool. Derivatives can ensure that some of the unpredictability that occurs in the financial market is hedged, or neutralized, at least to some degree. However, if derivatives are misused, they have the capacity to cause a great deal of damage.

Generally speaking, derivatives are used to protect certain positions, although they can also give you exposure to areas that the bank decides that it wants to have exposure to. With regard to speculation, I think it depends on the degree of speculation. Financial institutions are in the risk and reward business – to get the reward, they have to take a risk. So derivatives are another tool you can use to take risks – to expose yourself to risk in certain areas where you decide to do that.

POSSIBLE ANSWERS

1   Harrison says that they need to take risks.

2   1   Sinclair says 'they are not entirely new' which suggests that they are quite new, while Harrison says they 'have been around for a very long time, in various formats'.

   2   He means that they allow you to earn higher returns, but 'at the cost of big increase in risk'.

   3   If they have a bill coming up in the future that will have to be paid in US dollars.

   4   They are complicated, and banks and companies might not fully understand them.

   5   He means that they have a bad reputation and that a lot of bad things have been written about them in newspapers.

   6   'Give exposure' means to be in a potentially risky situation, e.g. if a price moves in an unexpected direction.

   7   He means that it is the nature of their business to take risks and (if they are successful) to be rewarded for them.

Reading 2: An investment 'time bomb'

This article is adapted from BBC News Online, 4 March 2003: http://news.bbc.co.uk/go/pr/fr/-/1/hi/business/2817995.stm.

Many learners will know about Warren Buffett, who runs the Berkshire Hathaway investment group. In 2006, his net worth was estimated at $46 billion, of which he planned to give 80% to good causes. There were three huge US bankruptcies between December 2001 and July 2002 – WorldCom, Enron, and Global Crossing – which partly explains the negative sentiment towards derivatives in the following years.

Before reading the text, learners could look at just the headline and make some predictions about the content.

ANSWERS
1 investment
2 clients
3 risk
4 instruments
5 speculate
6 commodities
7 underlying
8 hedge
9 contracts

Discussion

Derivatives can be described as 'weapons of mass destruction' because they can potentially result in huge and almost unlimited losses.

Buffett describes derivatives as a 'time bomb' because they run into the future and can be sensitive to market changes that are entirely unforeseen at the present.

As mentioned in the **Practice** section of the **Student's Book**, notable bankruptcies resulting from derivatives trading include Barings Bank, Orange County, Long-Term Capital Management, WorldCom, Enron and Global Crossing. Information about these bankruptcies is easily available on the internet.

After reading, learners can discuss whether they think Buffett's predictions are right – will there be another 'mega-catastrophic' bankruptcy in the near future?

Language focus: Clarifying, summarizing and paraphrasing

If the instruction in Question 2 to choose any of the odd-numbered units is too vague, select just one unit, and have the whole class work on the same tapescript.

Mark Twain's words of wisdom are from 'Pudd'nhead Wilson's New Calendar', appended to Chapter 56 of *Following the Equator* (1897). In the 1880s and 1890s, Twain lost over $200,000 investing in the development of a typesetting machine which was never commercialized, and had to undertake extensive journeys to earn money by giving lectures and writing about his travels.

Practice

Presentation language is introduced in **Units 22** and **24**; for the moment learners can prepare a short, informal talk (perhaps in pairs or groups). Learners will need time to prepare this and it could be set as homework. Remind learners that when they are listening to their colleagues' presentations, they should try to practise some of the language of clarifying introduced in the **Language focus**.

The dangers of derivatives are mentioned in the **Background** at the beginning of the unit.

20 Negotiating 2

To learn how to: deal with conflict; conclude successful and unsuccessful negotiations
To practise: negotiating working conditions

Lead in

It is commonly suggested that the four statements in column A describe business behaviour in the US: the boss decides, rather than seeking a consensus; conflict is seen as part of the negotiating process; the purpose of negotiating is to arrive at a binding written contract; and you can interrupt, say 'No', and be quite forceful. The statements in column B are more likely to be made by people from Asian or Arab cultures. These 'norms' are intended to promote discussion, and both teachers and learners are invited to add their own ideas.

Discussion

The aim of these questions is to draw out learners' experiences of negotiating and particularly any difficult situations which they have had to deal with, as this will help them with the context of the **Listening** exercise.

Vocabulary

ANSWERS
1e 2d 3c 4a 5b 6f

Listening 1: Concluding an unsuccessful negotiation

This is the negotiation that was discussed in the **Listening** activities and the role play in **Unit 10**. The learners may have chosen <u>not</u> to go ahead with the plan; here the bank is negotiating with an Indian company, but the negotiation fails.

An additional discussion question: is the bank being reasonable in insisting on only having experienced staff working in the call centre?

⊘ 20.1 TAPESCRIPT

Ajay Sharma: The major sticking point at the moment seems to be staff training. What exactly are your objections to our proposal?

Alice Hewlett: The problem is not with training so much as with staff retention. We are worried that the way the call centre industry is booming in India, and given the rapid staff turnover, our customers may be talking to people who are quite new to your company and who have not had enough training or experience with our products. We need some guarantees about the people who will be answering our customers.

Ajay Sharma: I think we both need to give a little ground here. What do you think is a reasonable solution?

Alice Hewlett: That you guarantee that all the employees answering our calls will have had at least three months' working experience with bank products.

Ajay Sharma: Well, I'm sorry, Mrs Hewlett, but we cannot do that. Perhaps we should adjourn to reconsider our positions? Hopefully we can come back with some fresh ideas.

Alice Hewlett: I'm sorry, but I don't think that would help. I've told you where we stand on this, and we can't change our position. And if you can't give us a guarantee on this, we'll have to look elsewhere. I'm afraid that we've reached a stalemate, so I think we should call it a day.

ANSWERS

1 1 The training and experience of the call centre staff.

2 The bank wants trained and experienced staff, but thinks there soon won't be enough because the number of call centres in India is expanding rapidly, and people do not usually work in them for very long.

3 He first suggests finding a compromise, which Alice Hewlett says is not possible, and then suggests adjourning to reconsider and maybe find some fresh ideas, which she says will not help.

2, 3 Answers to Question 2 are in italics – the other answers are for Question 3.

1	*What exactly are your objections to our proposal?* Could you explain exactly what the difficulties are? What is the underlying problem here?
2	*I think we both need to give a little ground here.* A compromise could be to …
3	*What do you think is a reasonable solution?* What would you suggest?
4	*Perhaps we should adjourn to reconsider our positions?* I think it would be a good idea to come back to this later. Let's have a break and perhaps we can come back with some fresh ideas.
5	*We'll have to look elsewhere.* I'm afraid we'll have to find another supplier.

Language focus: Dealing with conflict

ANSWERS
1b 2c 3a 4b 5c 6a 7c 8b 9c

VOCABULARY NOTE
Learners may not know the phrase *reach a stalemate*, originally from the game of chess.

Discussion

The aim of these questions is to help learners focus on more positive negotiating experiences in preparation for the next **Listening** activity.

Listening 2: Concluding a successful negotiation

This is the same situation as in the practice activity on conditional offers in **Unit 18**. For Question 3, learners could also look back at the summarizing phrases they had in **Units 12** and **Unit 19**.

⦿20.2 TAPESCRIPT
Representative of computer manufacturer: OK, we can agree to that. The option will run until the end of the year.

…

Can we just run through what's been agreed? We're going to deliver five hundred T650 workstations at $1,450 each, in fourteen days – which is to say, the twenty-third of May – with a payment period of 60 days. These workstations will be fully guaranteed for twelve months. And you have an option to buy two hundred more T650s at the same price until the end of the year.

…

I expect you'd like that in writing! We'll draw up a full contract. Well, I think we've both got a good deal. I hope this can be the basis for a long-term relationship.

Useful phrases

These phrases will be needed for the **Practice** activity at the end of the unit.

Listening 3: Saturday opening

This listening acts as a lead in and background information for the **Practice** activity.

20.3 TAPESCRIPT

Employee A: I saw the top secret 'Saturday report' today. It's going to happen.

Employee B: Not without negotiations with the staff association, it's not. So what are they planning?

Employee A: I can't tell you. I told you – it's confidential!

Employee B: Oh, come on.

Employee A: Well, OK. I think they're sending round a circular tomorrow anyway. So, they're planning to open most branches on Saturdays, from ten till two, and to stay open an hour longer on weekdays.

Employee B: And they think they're going to find enough volunteers to work on Saturday?

Employee A: Oh no, not volunteers. They want to change all our contracts, though of course not everyone will have to work at the weekend. At least, not every weekend.

Employee B: I don't believe it! What are they offering in return?

Employee A: Two hours off – a two-hour reduction in the working week for all staff who work on Saturdays. Though the new branches will be so nice, people won't want to work less!

Employee B: You must be joking!

Employee A: I am joking. And they're going to create 25 new jobs, or 50 part-time ones. And there'll be an annual bonus for all staff if sales of banking products increase with the longer opening hours.

Employee B: Yeah, but what if there isn't any increase in business, and customers just come in at a different time? On Saturday instead of during the week. There'll be no bonuses.

Employee A: They're convinced that won't happen.

Practice

See **pages 120** and **129** of the **Student's Book** for the file cards.

The short text sets the scene for the **Practice** activity. MGS Bank is the fictitious bank which has appeared throughout the book.

This is a negotiation between the bank's management and representatives of the Staff Association. There are just two roles, but unless you only have two learners, your learners will prepare and negotiate in two teams.

While preparing, learners could keep in mind the tips for negotiating from **Unit 18**. That is, before negotiating, each side should know exactly what it wants and what it will settle for, anticipate counter-proposals and compromises, and think about how it will react to them. Before they begin, you could remind the learners of their earlier answers concerning who makes decisions, whether conflict and disagreement are acceptable, and whether contracts are definitive, or should be changed to reflect changed situations (perhaps including extended opening hours).

How the negotiation proceeds, and whether an agreement is reached, will depend on the learners. There is room to move on both sides.

VOCABULARY NOTE

Hole-in-the-wall is a British and Australian name for a cash point or cash machine; Americans generally call it an *ATM*, short for *Automated Teller Machine*.

21 Asset management

AIMS

To learn about: asset and fund management; key vocabulary of asset management and allocation
To learn how to: disagree diplomatically
To practise: talking to a client about their investment portfolio

BACKGROUND: ASSET MANAGEMENT

Institutional asset managers invest the assets of pension funds, insurance companies, etc. Asset managers working independently or in private banks manage the portfolios of wealthy individuals and families. *Mutual funds* (also called *unit trusts* in Britain) invest money for small investors in a range of securities.

Asset managers have to decide how to allocate funds for which they are responsible:

- whether to invest in shares, mutual funds, bonds, foreign currencies, precious metals, etc.
- whether to diversify in a wide range of assets
- whether to try to accumulate capital, or to concentrate on capital preservation and the avoidance of risks
- whether to use an active strategy – buying and selling frequently, adapting the portfolio to changing circumstances, or a passive strategy – buying and holding securities, leaving the position unchanged for a long time
- whether to invest in an index-linked fund (*tracker fund* in the US) that simply follows the movements of a stock market index, or whether to try to 'beat the market', which – unsurprisingly – not many asset managers do.

The **Listening** and **Reading** activities in this unit give further information about asset management.

Lead in

The **Lead in** to **Unit 15** concerned speculation and stocks, but your learners may now be significantly wealthier because of the **Practice** activity in that unit!

Some learners may want to work as investment advisors, or already be working in this field. The third question, about asset management strategies, is answered in the subsequent **Listening** exercise.

Listening 1: Asset management and allocation

⊘ 21.1 TAPESCRIPT

Paula Foley: Asset management nowadays means managing financial assets – excluding real estate, works of art, and things like that. Individual portfolios and institutional funds are very different, because of size and objectives. There are many classes of possible investments in this area: bonds, stocks, cash, precious metals, funds and so on. Each of these classes contains a certain number, and sometimes a very large number, of sub-classes, like categories of bonds or international stocks of various countries.

The problems for managing assets in this area concern, first of all, the objectives of the portfolio, of the client, and its size. The objectives of a private portfolio will depend on whether you invest for retirement or for use in the next few years, for instance to buy real estate. Another major factor is size, because you can easily diversify and then steer a large portfolio, and it is sometimes much more expensive to do so for a small one. This problem of objectives and portfolio diversification has a direct impact on the returns which are needed or expected to meet these objectives and the implied risk of these portfolios, a risk which depends largely on the returns that are expected.

In practice, the two major questions which arise are first, defining a strategy and second, an investment style. The strategy in fact means asset allocation. You need to decide what proportion of the funds you will invest in those various classes: bonds, stocks and so on. The asset allocation is the key to the performance of the portfolio, whether it is between industries, between countries, or anything else. It is also the heart of the implementation of a reasonable diversification. But mind you, diversification can be overdone, and then it becomes a very expensive and unproductive exercise.

ANSWERS
1 Paula Foley does not mention derivatives, interest and liabilities.
2 1b 2c 3f 4e 5g 6a 7d

Listening 2: Investment styles

The aim of the second task is to pick out more detail from the interview. Learners will need to listen more than once.

⊙ 21.2 TAPESCRIPT

Paula Foley: The second point is style, which is very often not recognized by investors. There are a number of styles of investment management, the main ones being first of all, growth investment, which, as the word says, is looking for growth – for capital accumulation – and looks for growth companies in growth industries. The second is value, which is the opposite of growth, which is conservative industries with high asset values and stable or low-growing earnings.

The third main style is the choice between large and small companies, on the equity side. Large companies are supposed to be stable and more reliable; small companies very often give a faster rate of growth, but are more difficult to track and manage.

Another point here is when you have invested your funds, you still have to manage your portfolio, which may take up to a year to build up. There are essentially two ways to manage a portfolio. One is active management, where you buy and sell quite frequently, to adapt your

portfolio to your objectives, and to changing market circumstances. The other one is passive investment: you buy and hold, which used to be for many years, sitting on your positions, until things fundamentally changed or bonds came to maturity. This has now been developed into index-linked portfolios, which try to follow stock market or bond market indices, and replicate their movements. This can be a very attractive proposition, or not, considering that these portfolios go down with the market in negative times.

A final important remark is that portfolios which are composed of funds also need to be managed. You cannot buy and sit on a fund portfolio indefinitely. Funds change – they change their management, they change their quality and their objectives; therefore, just like an ordinary portfolio, a fund portfolio has to be managed too.

ANSWERS
1 She mentions three styles: growth investment, value investment, and the choice of large or small companies.

POSSIBLE ANSWERS
2 Growth investment means looking for growth or capital accumulation: companies that will get bigger.
Value investment is investing in big, stable companies in conservative industries with earnings that might grow slowly but won't fall.
Large companies are generally stable and more reliable than small ones.
Small companies often grow more quickly than large ones, but are more difficult to get information about.
Active management means you buy and sell quite frequently, adapting your portfolio to your objectives and changing market conditions.
Passive investment means you don't buy and sell frequently; you buy and hold, until bonds mature or the financial situation fundamentally changes.
Index-linked portfolios try to follow or copy the movements of stock or bond market indices or indexes.

Even fund portfolios need to be managed, as their managers can change, or their quality and objectives can change.

3 Common combinations that are used by the speaker are:
asset values
capital accumulation
conservative industries
growth investment
growth industries
investment management
stable earnings

NOTE

You could encourage your learners to make sentences with the combinations in Question 3, in order to help them learn them and to see how they are used.

Reading: Fund management

This text, from *The Economist*, 31 August 2002, pp. 51–2, is shortened and very slightly simplified.

The vocabulary explanations before the text should help with unfamiliar phrases which appear in the text. Learners may need some time to read and understand the whole text, so you may want to get them to read it paragraph by paragraph and answer the questions below as they go along. (For example, Question 1 is answered in the first paragraph, Questions 2 and 3 in the third paragraph, and so on.) Learners may find it easier to deal with this type of text in shorter 'chunks'.

POSSIBLE ANSWERS

1 Because they are not performing better than passive managers, who simply invest in indexed funds.

2 Because people argued that it was impossible to consistently do better than the markets (and they wanted to take advantage of the bull markets in the 80s and 90s).

3 The efficient-market hypothesis is that a company's share price always accurately reflects all available useful information. Further analysis will not reveal any additional information, so there is no way of knowing more than the rest of the market participants.

4 George Soros argues that markets often over- or undervalue things, and that high and low share prices can make things happen which in turn have an effect on prices.

5 Peter Lynch found good companies that the market was undervaluing.

6 Because most active managers do worse than the market average, and unlike passive managers they also charge fees.

Discussion

How long this discussion lasts will depend on the financial sophistication of the learners. People working in asset management departments should have quite a lot to say; those who are in other departments may have other opinions. Your learners might also have experience of the different types of funds which they could share.

Language focus: Using diplomatic language

Refer the learners back to **Unit 12** or ask them if they can remember any phrases for politely disagreeing or asking for opinions (especially when their opinion is different). You could also remind learners about the language for suggestions they looked at in **Unit 5**. They can use these phrases in the **Practice** activity.

Some general guidelines for making language more diplomatic in English:

- using 'softeners' (*perhaps, maybe,* etc.)
- changing negative adjective to 'not + positive' (e.g. sentence **c** below)
- using modals (*could, should, would, might*)
- using *I'm afraid* or *I'm sorry* (even if it's not your fault).

ANSWERS
1d 2a 3f 4c 5b 6e

Practice

See **pages 121** and **131** of the **Student's Book** for the file cards.

This activity will require the learners to use quite a lot of the language they have studied elsewhere in the book. The advisor (Role A) will not only need to be diplomatic (covered in this unit), but also suggest other options (**Unit 5**), make proposals (**Unit 18**), agree or disagree (**Unit 12**) and finally describe market trends (**Unit 13**). The client (Role B) will need to agree or disagree (**Unit 12**), accept or reject proposals (**Unit 18**) and describe a chart (**Unit 13** or **15**).

Learners can work in pairs or small groups to prepare their role (all advisors working together and all clients working together). When they have had time to prepare, different pairs can act out their dialogue. The other learners can listen and, if appropriate, decide which meeting has the most successful outcome.

Writing

Learners can refer back to **Unit 6** for standard letter-writing phrases as well as those for writing a letter of complaint.

POSSIBLE ANSWERS

1

> Dear Mr ----
>
> I am writing to confirm the suggestions I made at our meeting this morning.
>
> Because your savings constitute your retirement fund, it would be inadvisable to take any risks with the capital. Consequently I recommend retaining most of your positions in bonds, which pay an acceptable interest rate and are less volatile and risky than stocks.
>
> As you wish to invest in US stocks, I suggest that we wait until your £20,000 General Electric bond matures in six weeks' time, and then buy into a DJIA tracker fund.
>
> Could you please confirm by letter that you are happy with this arrangement.
>
> Many thanks

> Just a note to warn you that I expect one of my clients, Mr ----, to disagree with the positions I recommended to him this morning, and complain to the bank. He is self-employed and his capital constitutes his retirement fund, and is largely in high-quality bonds. However, he wants me to sell these and select US stocks and call options, as well as commodity futures. He also, illogically, wants to buy three-month US$ put options.
>
> I have explained to him that such an investment strategy would be inadvisable in his situation, and suggested putting £20,000 into a Dow-Jones tracker fund when one of his bonds matures shortly.
>
> Best regards

2

The Wealth Management Director
MGS Bank

...

Dear Sir

I am writing to complain about the person you have allocated to my account, Mr ----. For an investment advisor, he seems to know very little about asset management, and he ignores everything I say to him. I would have thought his role would be to listen to my requests, and to act on them.

I have a lifetime of professional experience in business and finance, and could quite easily transfer my account to another bank or even to a hedge fund. Furthermore, I could easily trade stocks and currency online without paying commissions to a bank.

Your advisor, Mr ----, does not seem to be competent to select stock and currency options and commodity futures, despite my telling him precisely what I want to do with my money. Consequently I would like someone more senior to take over responsibility for my account.

I look forward to hearing from you.

Yours faithfully

Dear Mr ----

I refer to your letter of 29 February 20--.

I can assure you that Mr ----, who is in charge of your account, is a highly qualified, experienced and successful investment advisor.

The investment strategy that he has recommended for your portfolio is entirely consistent with your profile as an investor. Given that your capital represents your only professional pension, it would be very unwise to take risks with it in the hope of accumulating more capital.

However, given your dissatisfaction with Mr ----, we will transfer management of your account to Mrs ----. She will shortly be contacting you by telephone.

We look forward to continuing to do business with you in the future.

Yours sincerely

---

22 Presentations 1

AIMS

To learn about: presenting skills, learning styles
To learn how to: structure a presentation; introduce a presentation; prepare visual aids
To practise: writing and giving the first part of a presentation

Lead in

Most people working in business occasionally have to give presentations of some description. At lower levels these are likely to be internal to the organization, to departmental colleagues or superiors – often in a meeting. The level of formality tends to rise when presenting to hierarchical superiors. At higher levels in an organization, people are increasingly likely to have to make external presentations in more formal settings, to clients, investors, etc.

Discussion

Most learners will have experience of presentations, as business students and at work. The aim of these questions and the speech bubbles is to get learners to think about the features of a good presentation, and how this can help them when they need to present in English. You could divide the class into two groups and ask group A to come up with a 'good presenters / presentation' list and group B a 'bad presenters / presentation' list.

POSSIBLE ANSWERS

Good presenters:

- Make well-planned presentations, with a clear, logical structure.
- State at the beginning how long they are going to talk, and stick to this.
- Check their equipment, the seating and the lighting before they start.
- Use visual aids (PowerPoint, transparencies on an overhead projector, etc.) with words and phrases, diagrams, charts and graphs that can be clearly seen by everybody.
- Make sure that what they say is relevant to the audience.
- Begin their presentation by explaining its content and purpose.
- Use visual aids or notes as a basis, but do not read a text.
- Speak loudly enough to be heard by everybody.
- Do not speak too quickly, and pause for emphasis when necessary.
- Make sure their presentations have a strong introduction and a strong conclusion.
- Signal the different parts of the presentation (covered in **Unit 24**).
- Look relaxed, positive and confident.
- Seem competent, organized and enthusiastic.
- Make a lot of eye contact with the audience.
- Move around and use their body (or at least hands and arms) to increase meaning.
- Welcome questions and answer them carefully (and look at the questioner).

Bad presenters:

- Don't check beforehand whether they can connect their laptop to the projector, and so perhaps find that they can't use their visual aids.
- Don't consider how the chairs are arranged or make sure that everyone can see.
- Don't consider light reflecting on the screen or the need to close the blinds and/or dim the lights.
- Begin a presentation without explaining its content and purpose.
- Read a written text.
- Speak so quietly that people at the back (or even the front) can't hear.
- Hesitate a lot and say 'Er ...' before every sentence.
- Look at the floor or the back wall instead of making eye contact with the audience.
- Use slides with words or diagrams that are too small to read or understand.
- Talk for longer than scheduled.
- Realize that they've run out of time, so suddenly end without summing up.
- Promise to answer questions at the end, but don't leave any time for them.

Reading: Learning styles

The idea for this questionnaire comes from a seminar by Marjorie Rosenberg. Some learners may be familiar with this notion, and be ready to discuss their learning styles. Others, who have perhaps never thought about this, may have less to say.

As the text says, most people use all three learning styles in different proportions, but many learners will select more statements in one box than the others. The point of this exercise – as well as allowing learners to think about their own preferred ways of learning – is to underline the importance of visual aids in presentations.

The word *kinaesthetic* may not be familiar, but it is the term generally used in this context. Some people suggest that presenters should provide pens and paper so that kinaesthetic learners can make notes.

ANSWERS
2 1b 2c 3a

Language focus: Visual aids

You can divide learners into two groups for this activity, with one group taking the first paragraph and the other taking the second.

POSSIBLE ANSWERS
2

> The introduction to a presentation usually
>
> - welcomes and thanks the audience
> - states the presentation's subject or title and its purpose
> - outlines the structure of the presentation
> - states how long the presentation will take
> - tells the audience when they can ask questions.

> The end of a presentation usually
>
> - signals that the speaker has nearly finished
> - briefly summarizes or repeats the main information
> - draws some conclusions
> - thanks the audience for listening
> - invites them to ask questions.

3 a a bar chart
 b a pie chart
 c an organization chart (or organigram)

Useful phrases

For Question 2, tell learners that there is not a phrase for every box in the table, so some boxes have more than one phrase. Others will be added after the **Listening** activity.

1	a	hesitate	d	save	g	have
	b	draw	e	see	h	feel
	c	going	f	take		
2	4	c, f	7	a, h		
	6	b, e, g	8	d		

NOTE

Telling your audience the length of your presentation is more or less standard practice (though unfortunately, actually sticking to that length is less so); this might require inexperienced presenters to practise their presentations in order to time them.

Listening: The introduction

This example of an introduction to a presentation uses portfolio strategies, discussed in **Unit 21**, as its subject matter.

🔘 *22* TAPESCRIPT

Paula Foley: Good morning everybody. Thank you all for coming today. My name is Paula Foley, and I'm Vice-President for Private Banking. This morning I'm going to talk about conservative portfolio strategies, because most of you are responsible for an increasing number of clients who choose this option. My presentation will take about fifteen minutes, and as you can see, I've divided it into four parts. The first part will be about risk management in general. The second part looks at diversification, which is of course the most important concept of all. Then I'll talk about the use of indexed funds, and finally I'll discuss capital preservation and capital accumulation. If anything isn't clear, or if you have any questions, please don't hesitate to interrupt.

OK. So, what is risk management? ...

POSSIBLE ANSWERS

1 1 Good morning, everyone.
   2 My name is ... and I'm the ...
   3 The theme of my presentation today is ...
      This morning I'm going to talk about ...
      The subject of my talk is ...
   4 My presentation will be in four parts.
      I've divided my talk into three parts.
      In the first part I'll talk about ...
      The second part is about ...

ANSWERS

2 1 She does all of these things.
   2 (Box 1) Good morning, everybody. Thank you all for coming today.
      (Box 2) My name is Paula Foley, and I'm Vice-President for Private Banking.
      (Box 3) I'm going to talk about conservative portfolio strategies, because ...
      (Box 4) My presentation will take about fifteen minutes
      (Box 5) I've divided it into four parts.
      (Box 6) and as you can see ...
      (Box 7) If anything isn't clear, or if you have any questions, please don't hesitate to interrupt.
   3 (Box 5) The first part ... , The second part ... , Then ... , ... and finally ...

3

> **Conservative portfolio strategies**
>
> • Risk management
> • Diversification
> • Indexed funds
> • Capital preservation and accumulation

Practice

See **page 136** of the **Student's Book** for the file cards.

There are three role cards with different presentation subjects for this activity. Help learners to choose a subject which is useful or interesting for them. The content of the talk being introduced here is not really important: the speaker only needs to mention the three or four parts of the talk that will be developed later. This exercise is about practising the elements of an introduction outlined in the previous exercises.

The learners could prepare this introduction out of class and present it in the following lesson – though with a large class, the learners are unlikely to want to hear and comment on more than three or four (very similar) introductions.

Ideally, the learners will be able to record their introductions, and listen to them afterwards.

The class can perhaps be invited to comment on the introductions, with reference to some of the following areas:

Did the speaker:
- include all the necessary parts?
- sound lively and enthusiastic?
- speak at the right speed?
- pause and hesitate (or say 'Er ...' or 'Um ...') too much?
- read too much?
- give the information clearly and simply?
- make eye contact with the audience?
- use appropriate gestures and body language?

It is probably a good idea to encourage the learners not to be too critical: presenting in public, especially in a foreign language, is difficult, and makes a lot of people very nervous.

23 Regulating the financial sector

AIMS

To learn about: financial regulation, managing conflicts of interest
To learn how to: use suffixes and prefixes
To practise: talking about conflicts of interest and ethical choices

BACKGROUND: REGULATING THE FINANCIAL SECTOR

Although, as discussed in **Unit 1**, the financial services industry was deregulated in the 1980s, a lot of regulations remain. Countries with a developed financial sector all have government agencies that regulate and supervise the industry, including the Financial Services Authority (FSA) in Britain, and the Federal Reserve (or the Fed) which supervises banks, and the Securities and Exchange Commission (SEC) which supervises corporations and the stock market, in the US.

There are regulations designed to prevent various practices that could lead to conflicts of interest – situations where what is good for one department is not in the best interests of another department and its customers. Examples of these include the following:

- banks selling securities they have underwritten to their retail customers

- banks writing research reports exaggerating companies' financial strength, in the hope of getting investment banking business from these firms

- auditing firms disregarding dubious accounting practices, in the hope of getting additional consultancy work from the companies whose accounts they audit

- people in banks' mergers and acquisitions departments doing insider trading or dealing – profiting from advance knowledge of takeovers.

See the **Reading** and **Discussion** sections in this unit, and the **Tapescript** of the interview with Steve Harrison.

Lead in

Discussing the Doonesbury cartoon (from 2002, after Enron, WorldCom and a number of other accounting scandals) is a way into this unit. Mike Doonesbury's teenage daughter Alex mistakes the newspaper's business pages for the crime pages. The cartoonist Gary Trudeau seems to be suggesting that there is a lot of financial crime going on, and that perhaps some of its perpetrators ought to go to prison. Do the learners agree?

Learners might be aware of the temptations or the possibilities that present themselves to various financial organizations, and the potential conflicts of interest that arise in business and finance (mentioned in the **Background** above). The second question asks whether learners have ever had any problems with financial institutions as customers. Asking them to talk about their professional experience would be more delicate.

Reading: Conflicts of interest

Learners who have some knowledge of the financial world or are already working in this sector will probably have more to say about these subjects. However, you can ask learners if they have heard of any scandals involving insider dealing as this is the subject of the fourth situation. Two of these situations (**a** and **c**) are also mentioned in the second **Listening** activity.

ANSWERS

1, 2

a   **Potential problem:** In the 1920s, some American banks sold such securities to their own customers, when this was obviously not the best possible investment for their customers (because there had to be a good reason why nobody else wanted the securities).

   Potential solution: To prevent commercial banks (with depositors) from underwriting securities, and only allowing investment banks to do this. In the US, the Glass–Steagall Act of 1933 did this. However, this act was repealed in 1999.

b   **Potential problem:** Banks competing to get investment banking business from companies might be tempted to issue research reports about these companies that exaggerate their financial strength, and in this way convince investors to buy their stocks. As mentioned in **Unit 1**, ten of New York's largest banks were fined a total of $1.4 billion for doing this in 2002.

   Potential solution: One of the provisions of the Sarbanes–Oxley Act, passed in the US in 2002, is that research analysts have to disclose whether they hold any securities in a company they write about, and whether they have been paid any fees by the company. However, this would not prevent researchers who are trying to get work from companies, who don't possess any of their shares and are not being paid by them, from writing inaccurate reports.

c   **Potential problem:** Auditing firms seeking consultancy work with the companies whose accounts they audit might be tempted to let their clients get away with what is known as 'creative accounting': using all the tricks and loopholes of accounting in order to hide losses or increase the declared profit.

   Potential solution: An obvious solution is for auditing firms to split off their consultancy department into an entirely separate business from the auditing firm. This was another of the provisions of the Sarbanes–Oxley Act.

d   **Potential problem:** This gives huge opportunities for insider dealing: buying or selling securities, and making a capital gain, on the basis of privileged information one has because of one's job.

   Potential solution: Most banks have what they call 'Chinese walls' surrounding departments that have confidential price-sensitive information. This means that no information should leave the department, and banks threaten tough penalties for people who reveal or use confidential information. But of course when information is leaked it is very difficult to prove who did it.

Vocabulary 1

ANSWERS

1   statutory
2   mandate
3   compliance
4   wholesale
5   counterparties
6   supervision

Listening 1: The Financial Services Authority

The interview with Steve Harrison returns to a subject discussed in **Unit 1** – the growth of financial conglomerates – and the regulatory response.

🔊 23.1 TAPESCRIPT

Steve Harrison: I think I'm correct in saying that the FSA came into existence on the first of June 1998. It was formed from nine organizations, I believe, although it may be slightly more now because extra responsibilities have been added to its mandate. The creation of the FSA was in recognition of developments taking place in the financial markets, the way firms were organizing themselves. The firms are not just banks any more, they're more like financial conglomerates, and so there needed to be a way to ensure that the supervision of these firms is appropriate.

The firms were becoming more and more integrated, and in order to make financial regulation more efficient, it was felt that the regulator in the United Kingdom should consider doing the same thing. So the decision was made to establish an integrated financial regulator incorporating all of those different elements.

When it's working with banks like ours, the FSA's main objective is to understand the institution, what it's currently doing and what it's seeking to do. The FSA is governed by statutory objectives such as protecting consumers and fighting financial crime. So that underpins all of its work. But the nature of its job, in relation to us, is to communicate with a wide range of people in the institution, both in our compliance department and at very senior executive levels. The FSA needs to understand our strategy as well as what we are doing on a day-to-day basis, in terms of our products and of how we are treating our customers. These customers may be consumers but they can also be what we would call wholesale counterparties – other banks that we deal with on a regular basis.

ANSWERS

1 Harrison mentions points 1, 2 and 4.

POSSIBLE ANSWERS

2 1 The FSA was formed as an integrated financial regulator in response to the growth of financial conglomerates.
   2 Protecting consumers and fighting financial crime.
   3 The bank's strategy and what they are doing on a day-to-day basis, concerning products and how they treat their customers.
   4 Other banks they regularly deal with.

Listening 2: Conflicts of interest

In this part of the interview, Harrison talks about conflicts of interest.

🔘 23.2 TAPESCRIPT

Steve Harrison: ... We need to recognize that there have always been conflicts of interest. The crux of the problem is not the fact that we have them, but the way in which firms manage these conflicts of interest.

Often it's about how you control information within financial institutions. Increasingly, different parts of the firm will interact with the same counterparty, but in different ways. For example, there has been a situation in the press regarding equity research, where research analysts have been used almost to promote investment banking. That's caused a number of problems because retail investors – certainly in the USA – have purchased shares in firms on the basis of the research analysts' recommendation. There has been a suggestion that the view the analysts gave on those firms was actually not their real view. Their private view was that the firms were not nearly as attractive as they stated publicly, but they made these statements because there was a chance that if they did, then the firm would give investment banking work to the bank. Statistics in the UK show that the number of buy recommendations on firms substantially outweigh the number of sell recommendations on firms, so clearly there is a balance to be achieved here.

There's also auditing. Certainly a number of auditing firms have realized that the set of skills that they have within the firm means they are often very well placed – and legitimately placed – to provide extra consultancy-style work. Again, that is not necessarily a problem – what needs to be monitored is how this is managed with respect to the relationship with the client of the auditor. But certainly I think it's fair to say that many auditing firms have recognized this conflict in recent years and have either separated their consultancy business from the auditing firm, or have used other techniques to manage the potential conflict of interest. One of those has been, for example, that when they appoint an auditor, many clients now deliberately state that they will not use that firm for consultancy work. They will use another auditing firm for their consultancy work.

ANSWERS

1 1 False: '… there have always been conflicts of interest … The crux of the problem is … the way in which firms manage these conflicts of interest.'

2 True: 'Often it's about how you control information within financial institutions.'

3 False: 'That's caused a number of problems because retail investors … purchased shares.'

4 True: '… because there was a chance that if they did, then the firm would give investment banking work to the bank.'

5 False: '… the number of buy recommendations on firms substantially outweigh the number of sell recommendations on firms, so clearly there is a balance to be achieved here.'

6 True: '… they are often very well placed – and legitimately placed – to provide extra consultancy-style work.'

7 False: '… many auditing firms have recognized this conflict in recent years and have … separated their consultancy business …' (There was no legal obligation, at least not in Britain.)

8 True: '… when they appoint an auditor, many clients now deliberately state that they will not use that firm for consultancy work.'

2 He mentions two of the situations (**b** and **c**) described in the earlier **Reading** activity.

3 This question is optional: as mentioned above, discussing actual conflicts of interest in the learners' organizations is a delicate issue, though some learners may have experiences they want to talk about.

ADDITIONAL WRITING ACTIVITY

Ask learners to look at the **Tapescript** of the interview with Steve Harrison and prepare some slides summarizing what he says about:
*   what the FSA is and what it does
*   which conflicts of interest commonly arise and what can be done about them.

Language focus: Word formation

You may want to put the examples from the **Student's Book** (the word family from *regulate*) on the board and show learners how the different types of words are formed and mention common prefixes and suffixes for nouns, opposites, adjectives, etc. (This is mentioned in the section under the box in the **Student's Book.**) You will also need to look at word stress and how it changes within some word families. If you want some basic rules about word stress, there is a section in *English for Business Studies* (Cambridge University Press, 2002) and in *Professional English in Use Finance* (Cambridge University Press, 2006).

Learners can work together in pairs or small groups to complete the table, using a good English–English dictionary to help them. You should mention that they will have more than one word for many of the boxes.

The second column mentions abstract nouns: these are nouns which refer to the subject, such as *accounting*, rather than the concrete noun, such as *accounts*.

VOCABULARY NOTES

The table gives both *-ize* (generally American English) and *-ise* (generally British English) spellings. Another adjective from *manage* is *managing* (as in *managing director*).

You should point out the negative meaning of *profiteer*, and the difference between *valueless* and *invaluable*. Also mention that *valuable* and *invaluable* have the same meaning.

ANSWERS

Verbs	Concrete and abstract nouns	Nouns for people or organizations	Adjectives	Negative adjectives
ac'count (for)	ac'counts ac'counting ac'countancy accounta'bility	ac'countant	ac'countable	'unaccountable
ad'vise	ad'vice advisi'bility	ad'viser / ad'visor	ad'visable ad'visory	'unadvisable / 'inadvisable
con'sult	con'sulting con'sultancy consul'tation	con'sultant	con'sultative con'sultatory	
'deal (with)	'deal, 'dealings	'dealer		
in'dustrialize / in'dustrialise	'industry industriali'zation / industriali'sation in'dustriousness	in'dustrialist	in'dustrial in'dustrialized / in'dustrialised in'dustrious	non-in'dustrialized unin'dustrialized
in'vest (in)	in'vestment	in'vestor	in'vested	
'manage	'management	'manager	'manageable mana'gerial	un'manageable
'organize / 'organise	organi'zation / organi'sation	'organizer / 'organiser	'organized / 'organised	dis'organized / dis'organised
'profit (from)	'profit profita'bility	profi'teer	'profitable	un'profitable
'value (e'valuate)	'value		valu'ation 'valuable	in'valuable 'valueless

Vocabulary 2

ANSWERS

1 consultant, management, unprofitable
2 industrialized / industrialised, investment
3 accountant, valuable / invaluable
4 advisable, consult
5 unmanageable, profiteers
6 managers / management, accountable
7 accounting, valuing
8 advisor / adviser, invaluable, valueless

ADDITIONAL WRITING OR SPEAKING ACTIVITY
You could ask learners to compose a paragraph or two, or a short dialogue, using as many of the words in the box as possible.

Discussion

1   Some people argue that *insider dealing* is a crime without a victim and therefore should not be illegal. It is true that if you buy stocks that have already been sold, no one is losing anything, but if your buying encourages others to sell, it can be argued that they are losing a future gain because you are exploiting privileged inside information.

2   This concerns what economists call the *political business cycle*: manipulating the economy for political or electoral advantage. Beginning a period in office with a couple of years of high interest rates and *austerity*, and then reducing interest rates and / or taxes and risking inflation in the run-up to the next election may help a government get re-elected, but is clearly not good for financial stability.

3, 4   These cases concern ideas that are often referred to in terms of *corporate social responsibility*, or the rights of stakeholders – all groups of people with an interest in a company – as opposed to stockholders or shareholders.

VOCABULARY NOTE

Case 1 uses the American English term *stocks* rather than the British term *shares*; Case 4 uses the British English terms *shareholder* and *Annual General Meeting*. The American English equivalents are *stockholders* and *Annual Meeting of Stockholders*.

24 Presentations 2

AIMS

To learn about: the parts of a presentation
To learn how to: end a presentation; deal with questions
To practise: making a complete presentation

Lead in

The answer to the first question is, apparently, less than ten minutes – even if the presenter is the best in the world and you are extremely interested in the subject. The second question is very subjective, but learners can be invited to discuss their opinions.

Discussion

Learners can look at these opinions and discuss them in pairs or small groups. Most people will probably agree with points 1, 3, 5 and 6. Some people may disagree with point 2 because if a subject is familiar it may be easier to prepare. Most people would probably disagree with point 4. The **Language focus** in this unit is designed to help learners with this aspect of presentations.

Listening 1: Parts of a presentation

Learners should be familiar with futures, options and swaps, which are covered in **Unit 19**. You could ask learners to look at the excerpts from the presentation and predict the phrases before they listen. They could then listen and check their answers.

⊚ 24.1 TAPESCRIPT

Paula Foley: ... OK, so as I said, first of all I'm going to talk about financial futures, before moving on to options. As you probably know, futures were first traded on ...

... That's all I need to say about futures, so that completes the first part of my talk. Now let's turn to options, which are this department's speciality ...

... That's all I'm going to say about options, so unless you have any questions let's move on to the third part of my presentation, which is about swaps. As I said in my introduction, these fall into two main categories: interest rate swaps and exchange rate swaps. I'll begin with interest rate swaps, which some of you ...

... So that was interest rate swaps. Now we come to exchange rate swaps, which are still an important derivative instrument, even after the introduction of the euro ...

ANSWERS

1 ... first of all I'm going to talk about ...
2 ... before moving on to ...
3 That's all I need to say about ...
4 Now let's turn to ...
5 That's all I'm going to say about ...
6 ... unless you have any questions let's move on to ...
7 Now we come to ...

Practice 1

In **Unit 22**, learners prepared the introduction to a presentation on one of a range of subjects. They should return to that subject and decide what the different sections will be. They do not need to talk about any of these subjects, but merely suggest sentences to begin and end each section. You could suggest that learners write the sentences to begin with, but that they would not want to read them out in an actual presentation.

Listening 2: The end of a presentation

This is the end of the presentation which learners heard in **Unit 22** on conservative portfolio strategy.

⦿24.2 TAPESCRIPT

Paula Foley: OK, that's all I have to say about capital preservation and accumulation, so now I'll just summarize my three main points again. A conservatively managed portfolio should be widely diversified; it should be expected to rise or fall in line with one or more major stock indices; and it's more important to preserve capital than to accumulate it. So, to conclude, I have two recommendations. Firstly, I think we need to diversify our clients' portfolios more widely, probably across more than one stock market. And, secondly, given the current volatility of the markets, I think we all need to pay more attention to preserving our clients' initial capital sums than to increasing them.

Thank you all for your attention. Does anyone have any questions or comments?

ANSWERS

1 1a 2c 3d 4b
2 She recommends that they diversify their clients' portfolios more widely (probably across more than one stock market). She also recommends that they pay more attention to preserving clients' initial capital sums than to increasing them.

Useful phrases

Learners could look at these in conjunction with the Tapescript for Listening 2 in order to highlight the key phrases for ending presentations. They will be able to practise these in the next activity.

Practice 2

Again, learners return to the presentation they started in **Unit 22** and continued in **Practice 1**, above. They will build up to a complete presentation in **Practice 3**, below.

The learners could do this in pairs or groups, with one or two presenting to the whole class.

Language focus: Dealing with questions and troubleshooting

You could ask learners if they have had experience of presenting in English and what they found easy or difficult about it. It is generally accepted that the question and answer session is difficult because you can't prepare for it. Technological problems can also cause difficulties and you could ask your learners for their experiences of this.

In some cultures, looking at the questioner is not considered polite, but in British and US cultures it is considered impolite not to do so.

The tips and example phrases in the **Student's Book** provide useful language and information.

The troubleshooting situations are intended to review a number of language areas which have been covered throughout the course. Encourage learners to look back through their notes, particularly at **Unit 10** (Chairing a meeting), **Unit 11** (Checking and clarifying), **Unit 19** (Clarifying), **Unit 20** (Dealing with conflict) and **Unit 21** (Diplomacy) to help them with their answers. They can prepare their answers in pairs or small groups and then you can discuss the best options with the whole class.

ANSWERS

1 1b 2c 3a 4b/c 5a/b

POSSIBLE ANSWERS

2 1 Hello everyone and thank you for coming. /
    Right, let's get started.

  2 Would you like to come to the front? /
    I'll try to speak up.

  3 I'm afraid we seem to have a technical
    problem. Can anyone help?

  4 I'm sorry, let me rephrase that. / Let me
    explain that again.

  5 I'm afraid I'm not in a position to comment
    on that.

  6 I'm sorry, I've forgotten the word. / I'm
    sorry, I've lost my train of thought.

  7 Sorry, I'm not sure if I've understood
    exactly.

  8 Could you keep your questions until the end,
    please? / I think it would be a good idea to
    come back to this later.

  9 Perhaps we can set this point aside until
    later, and move on?

Practice 3

In this final activity, learners can finish their
presentations. In order to give them enough time to
prepare, this would be best done for homework.

Ideally, if time permits, all the learners should give their
presentation in front of the whole class, followed by
questions or discussion.

This could even function as an oral exam, possibly with
two or three learners doing joint presentations.

Recording the presentations (either on audio or video)
and analysing them afterwards would be very useful.
Often learners have no idea how they sound in another
language and, although it can be a shock, it is a very
useful way of giving feedback. You would probably want
to give your students the recording to listen to on their
own, rather than in front of the whole class.

Thanks and acknowledgements

This book has been a long time in the making, so long that I need to thank no fewer than three long-suffering commissioning editors at CUP – Will Capel, Sally Searby and Chris Capper, without whom, etc. A very hands-on and hard-working editor and an inspired and meticulous copyeditor have also had a huge input into this course – Joy Godwin and Lyn Strutt. Five reviewers read early drafts and made lots of very useful suggestions – Hazel Allen, Susy Macqueen, Mike Reilly, Rosemary Richie and Alison Silver. Earlier still a number of people reviewed the original proposal: Ahmed Al-Tuhaini, Tim Banks, David Beesley, Fiona Dunbar, John Anthony Hall, Jessica Kou, Anthony Nicholson, Allen Santucci and Barry Siegel. My thanks go to all of the above, many of whom will willingly testify to my regular reluctance to accept very good advice.

Thanks are also due to Suzanne Williams of pictureresearch.co.uk for finding the photos, to Sophie Clarke, Michelle Simpson and Chris Willis at CUP, to Wild Apple Design for turning a drab manuscript into the attractive book you are holding, and to Sarah Hall for proofreading.

For the listening material I'd like to thank all the people who gave us their time and expertise (including some who did not make it to the final edit), particularly Peter Sinclair, Kate Barker, Gerlinde Igler, Rhys Roberts, Raymond Larcier and Aidan O'Connor. The recordings were produced and edited by Leon Chambers.

The author and publishers would like to thank:

Peter Sinclair, Gerlinde Igler, Kate Barker and Professor Raymond Larcier for the interviews.

Design and page layout by Wild Apple Design Ltd

Made in the USA
Lexington, KY
14 September 2015